Next? AI

How we got into AI era and where we are going with Artificial Intelligence

By **Martin Kuncicky**

ISBN 9798863625140

Martin Kuncicky
www.iamdad.cz

"It has become appallingly obvious that our technology has exceeded our humanity."

Albert Einstein

Content

Prologue

In the past, I've embarked on numerous literary journeys, delving into diverse subjects, meticulously weaving narratives together. Each unfinished writing has been a reflection of my passions, interests, and the curiosity that drives me. However, this recent endeavour stands out, not just because of its subject but due to the transformative tool that has accompanied me: Artificial Intelligence.

Before AI became a formidable ally in my writing process, the extensive research, data gathering, and structuring required immense effort. While the struggle was often rewarding, it was also time-consuming and, occasionally, overwhelming. Now, thanks to AI's formidable capabilities, those once-tedious tasks have transformed into efficient, streamlined processes. This has not only hastened the pace of my work but, more importantly, freed up cognitive space, enabling me to tap into deeper reservoirs of creativity. I've always believed in the transformative power of technology, and experiencing it firsthand in my craft has been nothing short of revelatory.

No journey, however, is undertaken alone. As I reflect upon this literary endeavour, I'm filled with gratitude for the unwavering support system that has been my anchor: my family and friends. Their encouragement, feedback, and, most importantly, their belief in me have been the wind beneath my wings. They've been the inspiration behind every word, every idea, fuelling my passion and drive.

Here's to the future, where we co-create, innovate, and inspire, hand in hand with our digital counterparts.

Introduction

In the digital era, the pulse of technology beats faster every day, and at its core lies Artificial Intelligence (AI). Today, it's hard to find an industry or sector that hasn't been touched by AI. From the smartphones in our pockets to the financial systems that power our economies, AI is not just a luxury but a necessity for modern living.

Living in the 21st century, we find ourselves in the midst of a digital renaissance—a period characterised by a surge in technological advancements that redefine our daily lives. At the heart of this transformation is Artificial Intelligence (AI). To grasp the depth and breadth of AI's influence, it's vital to first understand its historical trajectory and the nuances of its construction.

The concept of machines mimicking human intelligence dates back centuries, from ancient automatons to Alan Turing's seminal 1950 paper, "Computing Machinery and Intelligence". Over the decades, our ambition to craft intelligent machines has been unwavering, yet the realisation of this dream has only truly taken shape in recent years. This acceleration can be attributed to a confluence of factors—

improvements in computational power, the explosion of digital data, and significant advancements in algorithms.

To understand AI's profound impact, consider the following:

Smartphones: Around 80% of smartphones integrate AI. Beyond the obvious voice assistants, AI powers camera enhancements, optimises battery usage, and even assists in network connectivity1.

Economic Impact: AI's economic footprint is colossal. By 2027, we're looking at a global AI market potentially worth $266.92 billion. The broader economic infusion, from

/imagine A time-lapse showing AI's growth in various sectors over the decades.

productivity gains to new market creation, is expected to add $15.7 trillion by the end of the decade.

The omnipresence of AI is not just limited to numbers; it's interwoven into our daily experiences:

E-commerce: The online shopping revolution isn't just about convenience. AI's predictive analytics suggest products, optimise prices, and even help manage inventory.

Social Media: Each time we browse social platforms, AI-driven algorithms curate our feed, ensuring we stay longer and engage more.

Photography: Modern digital cameras, even those in smartphones, leverage AI to enhance image quality, adjust settings in real-time, and even recognise faces.

In the annals of human history, the idea of crafting intelligence is not a novel one. Ancient tales whispered of the Greeks and their mechanical wonders, of myths where intricate automatons moved with a semblance of life, stoking humanity's perennial fascination. In the torchlit chambers of alchemists, the dream of creating a homunculus, a tiny artificial human, persisted.

As centuries passed and the medieval age gave way to the renaissance, a new kind of luminary emerged. Ada Lovelace, with her poetic soul and analytical mind, gazed upon Charles Babbage's designs for his Analytical Engine. Rather than seeing mere numbers, she envisaged harmonies and rhythms, suggesting the machine might one day "compose elaborate and scientific pieces of music."

But it was the 20th century that saw the rise of a different kind of magician – the computer scientist. Alan Turing, with his genius and tragic narrative, wondered if machines could think, suggesting a test of their intelligence. If a machine could converse indistinguishably from a human, perhaps it was time to bestow upon it the title of 'intelligent.' Not long after, the likes of John McCarthy and Marvin Minsky not only envisioned but actively sought to make machines that could mimic the labyrinthine complexities of the human mind.

The tale then winds its way into our era, an age of unimaginable data and unbridled connectivity. Every digital footprint, every echo in the vast expanse of the internet, was a note in a grand symphony. This era promised not only to read the score but to understand, predict, and compose. Computing power, once the luxury of the elite, was now a boon available to eager young minds in dorm rooms and visionaries in bustling start-ups.

Yet, in this digital tapestry, 'AI' wasn't a singular thread. It was a spectrum. At one end, there were the diligent Narrow AIs, mastering one task with a precision unattainable by humans. Somewhere in the distant horizon of this spectrum, there were whispers of a General AI, a digital entity not bound by the constraints of single-task mastery but equipped with an adaptive, learning intelligence rivalling humans. And beyond that? A realm of Super-intelligence, an entity surpassing human intelligence, with potentialities both wondrous and terrifying.

Today, we live amidst AI's gentle hum. In hospitals, algorithms pore over medical images, sifting through pixels to spot anomalies. On bustling Wall Street, amidst the cacophony of traders, silent algorithms trade billions, optimising, predicting, and sometimes, faltering. Our nightly entertainment, the show we choose on a quiet evening, is often whispered into our ears by the unseen recommendation engines of streaming platforms.

But as the golden glow of AI's dawn stretches across our society, shadows emerge. Questions of biases encoded in silicon, of jobs fading into the annals of automation, and of an omnipresent digital eye watching, judging, and sometimes misinterpreting. With AI's promise also comes its peril.

This story is not just of a technology but of an epoch, a shift akin to the renaissance but borne out of bytes and algorithms. It is a tale of humanity's aspirations, achievements, and the dilemmas of playing with the very fabric of intelligence.

As you journey through these pages, let's unravel this intricate dance of humanity and its digital progeny, exploring the wonders and the quandaries of the age of artificial intelligence.

Human history has been defined by its incessant quest for understanding, mastery, and innovation. The stories of our past are punctuated with monumental leaps of intuition, remarkable discoveries, and the creation of tools that have shaped our destiny. Today, as we stand on the cusp of an era dominated by AI, we embark on yet another odyssey—a journey that promises to redefine our future even as it connects us to our collective past.

In order to fathom the breadth and depth of this emerging universe, we've woven together an intricate tapestry in the pages that lie ahead. Spanning the gamut from the philosophical to the technical, from the origins of AI to its foreseeable future, this book is an exploration, an exposition, and a guide.

The vast expanse of our AI journey is delineated into three main realms:

1. The Philosophical Roots and Historical March

Every technological marvel of today has its roots anchored deeply in the annals of history, often beginning not with machinery or calculations, but with stories, aspirations, and the limitless scope of human imagination. Our journey commences by stepping back in time, traversing the millennia where humanity first toyed with the ideas of automatons, animated beings, and replicas of human intellect and consciousness.

This section draws from myths of civilisations long past—Grecian tales of Hephaestus crafting automated beings or the Jewish lore of the Golem. We'll journey through the halls of history, witnessing Da Vinci's pioneering inventions, weaving through the scientific fervour of the Enlightenment, and marvelling at the dawn of computing with figures like Ada Lovelace and Charles Babbage. Each chapter is an era, each page a testament to humanity's timeless ambition to craft intelligence.

2. Deciphering the AI Enigma

Transitioning from the past to the intricacies of the present, our second realm immerses readers into the mechanics and mysteries of AI. It's here that the nebulous concept of AI starts taking tangible form. Diving beneath the surface, readers will navigate the dense waters of algorithms, neural pathways, and layers upon layers of data processing.

We initiate this leg of the journey by building foundational knowledge—understanding the principles of programming, the languages that power AI, and the theoretical concepts that underpin machine intelligence. Gradually, the chapters evolve in complexity, unfurling the intricacies of Machine Learning, Neural Networks, and Deep Learning. By this section's culmination, you'll be privy to the inner sanctums of

AI, a privilege previously reserved for experts and specialists.

3. AI: The Beacon of Tomorrow

Having scaled the peaks of the past and navigated the intricacies of the present, we finally set our sights on the shimmering horizon of the future—a future where AI holds the potential to either be our most empowering ally or a challenge we must surmount.

This segment emerges from the realm of theory into the bustling streets of our AI-driven world. It paints a picture of a world where medical diagnoses are a matter of milliseconds, where traffic jams are tales of yore, and where art and creativity have new, non-human maestros. However, it's not just a celebration of AI's potential; it's a deep introspection into the ethical quagmires, societal implications, and the philosophical conundrums that AI introduces.

4. The Grand Convergence

In "The Grand Convergence," the last ten chapters delve into the intricate dance between AI and humanity, examining our ever-evolving relationship. We begin by exploring the societal integration of AI, highlighting its profound implications for education, healthcare, and the very fabric of human interactions. As we move deeper, chapters unfold the ambitious vision of merging biology and technology, reimagining governance with AI as civic collaborators, and the tantalising quest for immortality. The narrative then shifts to a cosmic scale, pondering humanity's place in the vast universe and contemplating a future where AI might be our legacy. As the chapters culminate, they beckon readers to reflect on the potential futures that await, urging a harmonious coexistence with AI, all while emphasising the eternal value of human spirit and creativity.

The essence of these chapters lies not just in the marvels of technology but in the philosophical and ethical dilemmas they raise. From debating the nature of consciousness in a digitised world to pondering our responsibilities as creators and explorers of the cosmos, the narrative invites introspection. It paints a picture of a world where boundaries between man and machine blur but also serves as a reminder of the timeless human values and aspirations that should guide this intertwined journey. The Grand Convergence is more than a tale of technological marvel; it's a reflection on the essence of humanity in an AI-driven cosmos.

With every chapter, you will be accompanied by vivid illustrations made by AI itself,. These elements are more than mere adornments—they're designed to illuminate, elucidate, and enhance the narrative journey.

As you delve deeper into this tome, you won't merely be reading; you'll be reflecting, questioning, understanding, and imagining. This book is a commitment to a journey—an odyssey filled with wonder, knowledge, challenges, and possibilities.

So, as we turn the first page and take our initial step into the vast forest of AI, I invite you to not just read but to ponder, to challenge, and to dream. After all, it's not just a journey through the world of AI; it's an exploration of our past, a reflection on our present, and a speculation about our shared future.

To the odyssey of understanding, wonder, and co-creation, welcome aboard.

PART 1

The Philosophical Roots and Historical March

The Birth of a Dream

As our story unfolds, we find ourselves beneath the Grecian sun, where golden beams kiss the cobalt waves of the Aegean Sea. On a nearby island, the blacksmith god Hephaestus, if legend is to be believed, had fashioned beings of bronze. One particular tale spoke of Talos: a gargantuan automaton guardian, veins coursing with molten ichor. He patrolled the island's shores, repelling invaders with fiery breath and a strength no mortal could match.

On another leaf of the page, an illustration catches the eye. It's the depiction of Pygmalion, the sculptor king of Cyprus. Distraught by the flaws of mortals, he sculpted Galatea, a statue so exquisite, so lifelike, he found himself falling in love. The legend narrates how Aphrodite, moved by his adoration, breathed life into the statue, turning cold marble into warm flesh. Here was the first inkling of mankind's dream: to breathe life into the lifeless, to craft sentience from insentience.

The scents of olive and wine begin to fade as the narrative winds its path from Greece, through the hushed corridors of Alexandria's Great Library, and onward to the gilded streets of the Islamic Golden Age. A stopover in the House of Wisdom in Baghdad reveals scholars like Al-Jazari, who penned the "Book of Knowledge of Ingenious Mechanical Devices." An illustration depicts a water-powered clock, a mechanical marvel of its age, replete with moving figures and intricate gear mechanisms.

Emerging from the desert sands, our journey transports the reader to the cobblestone streets of Renaissance Italy. Suddenly, the pages come alive with a burst of colour and sketches. At the heart of it all is Leonardo da Vinci, the quintessential Renaissance Man. His curious mind envisaged machines that could fly, dive, and even, perhaps, think. Intricate illustrations sprawl across the pages, mirroring Leonardo's own journals. An ornithopter here, a robot knight there, and amidst them, the delicate swirls of the Vitruvian Man, epitomising the blend of art and science.

Yet, for all of Leonardo's brilliance, it was the dawn of the Industrial Revolution that truly birthed the precursors to modern computation. As the scent of burning coal and the cacophony of steam engines fill the narrative, another figure emerges from the shadows: Charles Babbage.

Amidst the fog-laden streets of Victorian London, Babbage, often dubbed the "father of the computer," dreamt of machines that could flawlessly carry out calculations. An expansive illustration dominates the next pages, revealing the majestic design of Babbage's Analytical Engine. Gears, levers, and spools intricately entwined, a symphony of brass and iron, awaiting the whisper of Ada Lovelace, the Enchantress of Numbers.

Ada's vision for Babbage's machine transcended mere calculations. With poetic grace, she noted how it might compose music, produce art, and perhaps, with the right

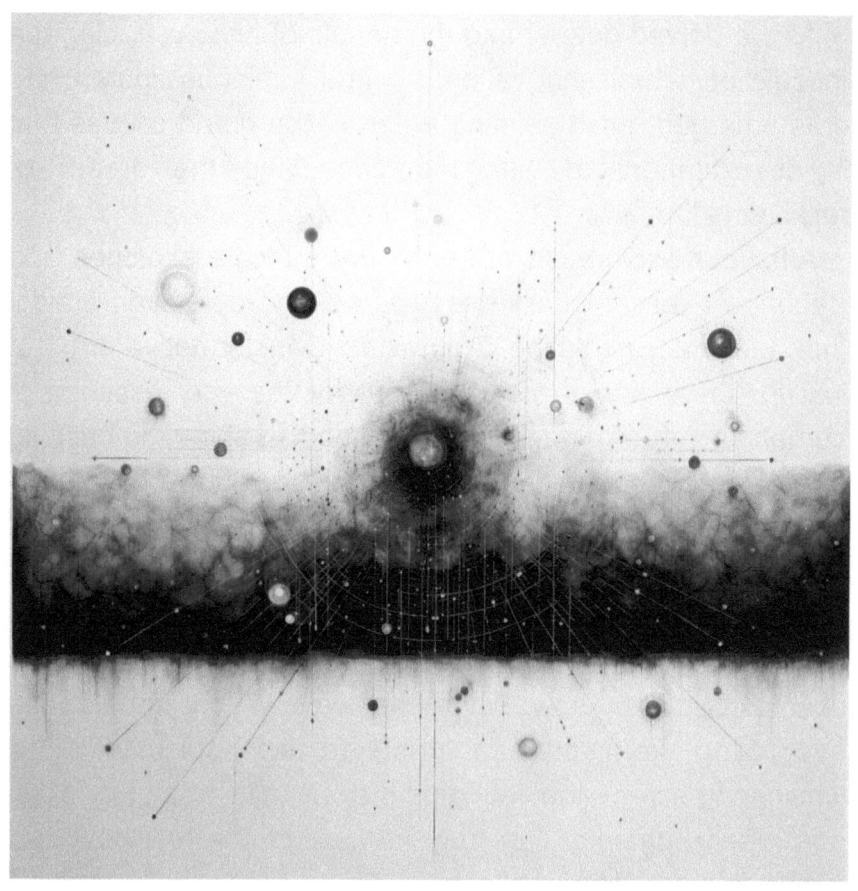

/imagine An expansive cosmos with stars (algorithms) connected by shimmering lines of matter (data).

algorithms, mimic thought processes. An adjacent illustration shows Ada, quill in hand, engrossed in her notes, surrounded by ethereal sequences of numbers transforming into notes, sketches, and patterns.

From the myths of Grecian gods to the mechanical wonders of the Renaissance and the dreams of Victorian pioneers, the journey has only just begun. The age-old quest to replicate life and thought has set the stage for even greater wonders, challenges, and innovations.

As we delved deeper into the annals of history, tracing the mosaic of human innovation, several luminous figures and eras emerged, each painting a part of the grand canvas that is our relationship with machines and the dream of replicating life.

After our exploration of Da Vinci's intricate sketches and Babbage's revolutionary designs, we find ourselves amidst the Industrial Revolution. This was a transformative era, not just for the world of machines but for the very essence of human society. A detailed illustration could show the bustling streets of 19th-century London, a juxtaposition of progress and poverty, as smokestacks towered over cramped alleyways.

The steam engine, a marvel of its time, was the heart of this revolution. James Watt and George Stephenson championed this powerful technology, which transformed everything from manufacturing to transportation. The whispering steam, the chugging pistons, all told a story of an age when humanity first truly harnessed the raw power of nature in a machine.

But the Industrial Revolution was more than just machines. It gave birth to the modern factory system, to urbanisation, and to a new class - the industrial proletariat. Here, we find the seeds of modern capitalism and the genesis of contemporary socioeconomic structures. A vivid illustration could encapsulate this transformation: a serene pastoral landscape gradually giving way to the industrial sprawl, symbolising the tectonic shifts of the era.

Parallel to this material transformation ran a stream of philosophical evolution. The Enlightenment era saw luminaries like Descartes, Kant, and Newton challenge the orthodoxy and reshape the boundaries of knowledge. The mechanistic view of the universe posited by thinkers like Descartes directly influenced our perception of machines. If the universe itself operated like a grand machine, governed by laws and principles, could life itself be replicated mechanically?

Mary Shelley's "Frankenstein" elegantly grappled with this question, exploring the limits of human ambition and the ethical implications of creation. An illustration here could depict the pivotal moment Dr. Frankenstein beholds his creation, capturing the dichotomy of wonder and horror.

As the 19th century waned, a new revolution was brewing, not in the factories but in the realm of communication. Samuel Morse's telegraph shrunk the world, making instant communication possible across continents. The Morse Code, a series of dots and dashes, can be seen as a precursor to the binary language of modern computers.

The close of the 19th century also bore witness to Nikola Tesla's and Thomas Edison's electrifying rivalry. Their battle over AC and DC not only transformed the energy landscape but also laid the foundation for the electronic age that would dawn in the next century. An illustration might depict the iconic moment when Tesla illuminated the 1893 Chicago World's Fair, marking the triumph of alternating current.

Amidst these technological marvels, the world of mathematics and logic was undergoing its own renaissance. George Boole introduced Boolean Algebra, an innovative system of logic that would later become fundamental to the design of electronic circuits and modern computing.

A large, evocative illustration captures the zeitgeist of the turn of the century. The world stands on the brink, with steam engines giving way to electric dynamos, horse carriages making room for automobiles, and handwritten letters being

17

replaced by telegrams. The dreams of replicating life and thought, which once resided in myths and sketches, now find a home in tangible machines and circuits.

Thus, this introduction serves as a bridge, connecting the ancient world's dreams and aspirations to the modern age's realities. The narrative underscores that every era, every innovation, is a stepping stone, gradually building the path to the world we inhabit today. The dream of creating, of emulating life and thought, has been an ever-present beacon, guiding humanity through the annals of time.

Evolution Follows

The dawn of the 20th century brought with it an age of profound upheaval and transformation. Nations clashed, empires fell, but from the smoky ruins of two World Wars, an unexpected phoenix began to rise: the age of electronics and computation.

Alan Turing, a figure whose brilliance was matched only by his tragic end, emerged as a beacon in this new era. As World War II raged and codes became the concealed language of warfare, Turing and his team at Bletchley Park devised the Bombe – a machine to decipher the enigmatic Enigma code of the Nazis. An accompanying illustration showcases the complexity of the Bombe, wires crisscrossing in a myriad of connections, evoking the very synapses of the human brain.

But Turing's dream extended beyond the immediacy of war. He pondered upon a universal machine, a computational entity that could emulate any conceivable mathematical process. This wasn't just an engineer's fantasy; it was a philosopher's dilemma. Turing's famous question, "Can machines think?", led to his conceptualisation of the Turing Test. A simple yet profound metric: if a

21

/imagine Alan Touring complexity of the Bombe, wires crisscrossing in a myriad of connections, evoking the very synapses of the human brain.

machine's behaviour is indistinguishable from a human, can we deny its intelligence?

The post-war years brimmed with optimism. The world witnessed the birth of ENIAC, the first general-purpose electronic computer. Vast and intimidating, it filled entire rooms, its vacuum tubes glowing like a cityscape at night. A detailed figure portrays ENIAC's vastness, with operators standing like minuscule figures, dwarfed by the machine's grandeur.

From ENIAC's monolithic stature, the narrative transitioned to the silicon revolution of the 1960s. Jack Kilby and Robert Noyce, almost simultaneously, championed the integrated circuit. Silicon Valley, once a literal reference to Santa Clara's geography, metamorphosed into a synonym for innovation. Readers can visualise the transition through a vibrant illustration.

By the 1970s and 1980s, computers transitioned from government labs and elite universities to our homes and

/imagine transition through a sprawling valley transforming into a bustling tech city, where orchards give way to server farms.

offices. Apple's Steve Jobs and Microsoft's Bill Gates became household names. A dual-page spread showcases a young Jobs unveiling the Apple I in a garage, juxtaposed against Gates showcasing Windows, symbolising the era's entrepreneurial spirit.

The narrative then sweeps into the 1990s, the age of the Internet. What began as a defence project, ARPANET, evolved into the World Wide Web. Tim Berners-Lee's invention transformed the computer from a standalone machine to a portal, connecting humanity in an unprecedented global network. An illustration paints a globe, with golden threads of connection weaving across continents, each thread pulsating with information.

As the new millennium dawned, the data generated was prodigious. Every click, every swipe, became a part of this digital fabric. This vast ocean of data required new ways of understanding, leading to the resurgence of artificial intelligence. Companies like Google, Facebook, and Amazon began harnessing sophisticated algorithms, driving recommendation engines, virtual assistants, and predictive analytics.

Deep learning, a concept once relegated to academic papers, became the linchpin of modern AI. Neural networks, inspired by the human brain, began making decisions, recognising patterns, and even creating art.

Present day: Now we stand at the precipice of a new age. AI isn't just a tool; it's a companion, a collaborator. Smart cities, autonomous vehicles, virtual realities - the line between the physical and digital is blurring. Elon Musk's Neuralink proposes merging the human brain with AI, while Sophia, the humanoid robot, ponders existential questions.

Yet, with the promise comes the peril. Ethical quandaries emerge: job displacements, data privacy, and the potential loss of what makes us inherently human. The current era is a tapestry of potential and pitfall, and it's upon us to navigate this labyrinth.

Continuing from the present, where we find ourselves ensnared in the intricate web of artificial intelligence, the evolution of this relationship between man and machine has profound implications not just technologically, but philosophically, ethically, and sociologically.

The dawn of the 21st century saw the rapid democratisation of information. The Internet, once a privilege, became a right. As handheld devices proliferated, connecting to the vast reservoir of global knowledge was only a touch away. Platforms like Wikipedia and Khan Academy democratised learning, while services like YouTube turned ordinary individuals into international celebrities overnight.

The meteoric rise of social media in the early 2000s redefined communication and human relationships. Facebook, Twitter, Instagram, and later TikTok, transformed how we interact, consume news, and even influence global politics. However, beneath these platforms' user-friendly interfaces lay sophisticated algorithms, continually learning, adapting, and predicting human behaviour. With every like, share, or tweet, AI systems were compiling comprehensive user profiles, tailoring content to keep users engaged longer.

But why this drive to retain users? The adage, "If you're not paying for the product, you are the product," became chillingly relevant. Digital advertising became a trillion-dollar industry, powered by AI's capacity to target users with unprecedented precision. An accompanying illustration might depict a user surrounded by digital advertisements, each tailored to their preferences, showcasing the eeriness of such accuracy.

This level of personalisation wasn't limited to advertisements. Streaming giants like Netflix and Spotify employed recommendation engines, offering shows and music based on users' past preferences. Here, AI's magic was more benign, helping discover a forgotten 80s track or a riveting documentary. But the underlying principle remained the same: understand the user, predict their preferences, and keep them engaged.

Simultaneously, the gaming industry underwent its renaissance. Gone were the days of pixelated characters and linear storylines. Games like Red Dead Redemption, Cyberpunk 2077, and the Final Fantasy series, boasted of expansive open worlds and characters powered by AI. Their decisions, relationships, and narratives adapted to each player's actions, offering a uniquely personal experience. The line between player and game blurred as virtual realities became almost indistinguishable from our own.

However, it wasn't all entertainment and engagement. The healthcare sector saw revolutionary advances, thanks to AI. Machine learning algorithms assisted radiologists in spotting tumours in X-rays, reduced drug discovery times, and predicted patient deteriorations in real-time. Wearable devices monitored vital statistics, offering insights into potential health issues even before they manifested physically.

In agriculture, AI-driven drones analysed soil quality, optimised irrigation, and monitored crop health, ensuring better yields and sustainable farming. Meanwhile, in finance, algorithmic trading predicted market movements with astonishing accuracy, while chatbots handled customer queries, often indistinguishably from human operators.

The transport sector, too, stood on the brink of revolution. Companies like Tesla, Waymo, and Uber championed autonomous vehicles. Prototype illustrations show sleek cars without steering wheels, using Lidar and intricate sensor systems, navigating bustling cityscapes with pinpoint accuracy. The dream of a driverless future, once the stuff of science fiction, was palpably close.

Yet, with these rapid advancements, ethical challenges began surfacing. AI's capability to synthesise information led to the advent of deepfakes, where videos of real individuals saying or doing things they never did became disturbingly convincing. The implications for misinformation, politics, and personal privacy were staggering.

Furthermore, biases in AI systems, often mirroring societal prejudices, became a significant concern. AI systems employed in criminal justice exhibited racial and socio-economic biases, while facial recognition systems struggled to identify individuals from certain ethnic backgrounds, leading to false arrests and widespread criticisms.

Additionally, the potential job displacements due to AI became a hotly debated topic. Would AI systems render entire professions obsolete? Or would they give rise to newer, hitherto unimagined career paths?

The philosophical implications were just as profound. If AI systems could compose music, paint masterpieces, or even write novels, what did it mean for human creativity? Was it the sole domain of mankind, or could silicon share this sacred space?

This continued acceleration towards an AI-dominated future begs introspection. Our story, rich with the tapestries of ancient myths, Renaissance innovations, industrial revolutions, and digital transformations, is at a crossroads. As we stand on the precipice, looking ahead, the choices we make now will define not just our future, but the essence of what it means to be human.

In this context, understanding our past becomes vital. The journey from Hephaestus's bronze guardians to Turing's universal machines and Musk's neural dreams is more than a technological evolution. It's a testament to humanity's insatiable curiosity, boundless creativity, and the perennial quest for transcendence. As we chart our path forward, it's this rich legacy that will be our guiding star, ensuring that in the dance of man and machine, humanity's soul shines the brightest.

Digital Symphony

At the close of the 20th century, the world stood on the precipice of a new era. While the innovations of the past laid the foundational stones, a magnificent digital symphony was about to commence, orchestrated by machines and algorithms, turning notes of binary into melodious wonders of the modern age.

The prelude to this symphony was the birth of the silicon chip. Integrated circuits, etched onto wafer-thin slices of silicon, promised capabilities hitherto deemed impossible. The Moore's Law, proposed by Gordon Moore, co-founder of Intel, observed that the number of transistors on a microchip would double approximately every two years, leading to an exponential growth in computing power while costs plummeted. A graph illustrating Moore's Law could show the striking rise of transistor count juxtaposed against the decreasing cost, capturing the spirit of relentless innovation.

The advent of the personal computer democratised this power. Figures like Steve Jobs and Bill Gates emerged as maestros of this digital era. Apple's groundbreaking Macintosh and Microsoft's ubiquitous Windows operating system brought the magic of computing into homes and offices. No longer were computers the exclusive domain of large corporations and government research labs. A poignant illustration here might depict a family gathered around their first home computer, wonder and curiosity evident in their eyes.

Yet, this digital symphony's true crescendo was the birth of the Internet. A vast, interconnected web of information, the Internet transformed the world in ways that even visionaries of the past couldn't have fathomed. Sir Tim Berners-Lee, while working at CERN, devised the World Wide Web, a system of interlinked hypertext documents accessed via the Internet. An interactive graph might illustrate the exponential growth of websites from the '90s to the present day, a testament to the digital explosion.

E-commerce platforms like Amazon and eBay opened global marketplaces to everyday individuals. A quaint illustration could capture a small-town artisan selling their handcrafted goods to a customer across the ocean, emphasising the Internet's power to bridge distances and create opportunities.

This interconnectedness also heralded the dawn of social media. Platforms like Facebook, Twitter, and later Instagram, transformed communication. They were more than just platforms; they were digital continents, each with its unique culture, norms, and ethos. One could imagine an engaging graphic here, depicting the world map with digital continents representing each major social media platform, emphasising their global influence.

Search engines, particularly Google, emerged as the guiding lights of this vast digital ocean, providing users with the tools to navigate and extract meaningful information. The PageRank algorithm, conceptualised by Larry Page and

/imagine Hands arranging puzzle pieces, with some forming discernible patterns while others remain scattered.

Sergey Brin, became the backbone of this digital navigation. A flowchart detailing the basics of this algorithm, with nodes and connections, might offer a glimpse into the complex machinery working behind every search query.

The field of entertainment underwent a renaissance. Platforms like Netflix and Spotify harnessed sophisticated recommendation algorithms to curate content, turning casual users into binge-watchers and avid listeners. Gaming, too, evolved from pixelated arcades to expansive, immersive worlds. Here, a split-screen graphic might contrast an early game like 'Pong' with the intricate landscapes of a modern game like 'The Witcher 3', highlighting the leaps in graphical fidelity and storytelling.

However, this digital age wasn't without its challenges. Cybersecurity emerged as a significant concern. Hackers, once relegated to pop culture stereotypes, became pivotal players in a global chess game of data and privacy. A graphic could depict a stylised lock being picked, symbolising the vulnerability of digital assets.

The torrent of data generated by the digital populace led to the rise of Big Data. Companies and governments now had access to vast troves of information, leading to groundbreaking insights but also raising ethical dilemmas about privacy and surveillance.

Amidst these sweeping changes, a new dream was taking root: Artificial Intelligence. While its seeds had been sown earlier, the 21st century's computing prowess and data abundance provided fertile ground for its growth. Neural networks, deep learning, and machine learning became buzzwords, promising a future where machines wouldn't just compute but 'think'. An illustrative figure could compare the human brain's neural network with an artificial neural network, drawing parallels and contrasts.

We find ourselves in a world where the boundary between the physical and digital is blurring. Cryptocurrencies challenge traditional notions of value and trust, virtual realities offer escapes from the mundane, and AI assistants like Siri and Alexa become part of our daily lives.

The Digital Symphony continues to evolve, its notes and melodies echoing the dreams, aspirations, challenges, and triumphs of humanity in the digital age. As we stand in this symphonic nexus, the past's echoes and the future's whispers harmoniously converge, crafting an anthem of human innovation and tenacity.

The 21st century had only just begun, and already, the music of the digital realm was evolving at a breathtaking pace. New instruments in this symphony emerged while older ones found renewed relevance, each contributing to a rich and harmonious tapestry of technological innovation.

In the early days of computing, storage was an expensive and finite resource. The floppy disks of yore, capable of holding a mere few megabytes, gave way to CDs, and then DVDs, each leap representing a significant increase in storage capacity. Yet, the true revolution came in the form of cloud computing. Companies like Amazon with its AWS, Microsoft's Azure, and Google Cloud proposed a paradigm shift: Why store data on personal devices when it can be kept on massive, decentralised servers, accessible anytime, anywhere? This move towards the cloud changed the very nature of business infrastructure and personal data management. A series of illustrative graphics might show the evolution of storage devices, contrasting their physical sizes with their capacities, culminating in the ethereal 'cloud' - a testament to the intangibility of modern data storage.

The ubiquity of smartphones further propelled this digital age. Companies like Apple with its iconic iPhone, and later, a multitude of Android devices, transformed the phone from a mere communication device to an indispensable life tool. These devices housed cameras, GPS, and a myriad of sensors, enabling applications that could have been considered magic in earlier eras. Augmented Reality (AR) and Virtual Reality (VR) started stepping out from the pages of science fiction into tangible experiences. Pokémon GO's meteoric rise could be a noteworthy case study, an AR game that bridged digital creatures with physical locations, making neighbourhoods battlegrounds and landmarks treasures.

Yet, beneath the sheen of the touchscreens, a transformation was underway in how software was crafted. The Open Source movement, championed by figures like Linus Torvalds, creator of Linux, posited that software's source code should be freely available. This wasn't just a technical decision but a philosophical stance, advocating for collaboration, transparency, and community-driven development. A side-by-side text comparison could illustrate the differences between proprietary and open-source code, highlighting the annotations and modifications made by diverse contributors in the latter.

E-commerce's rise was just one facet of the digital economy's explosion. The gig economy emerged, challenging traditional notions of employment and workspace. Platforms like Uber, Airbnb, and Upwork disrupted transportation, hospitality, and freelancing sectors, respectively. Here, a multi-panel illustration might depict a day in the life of a gig worker, from picking up morning ride-shares, working on freelance projects in the afternoon, to renting out their spare room in the evening.

Parallel to these advances, concerns grew about the digital world's environmental impact. Cryptocurrency mining, for instance, consumed vast amounts of electricity, rivalling the energy consumption of entire countries. E-waste, discarded electronic devices, became a pressing concern, with landfills brimming with obsolete gadgets. Infographics might starkly present these environmental costs, perhaps juxtaposing the energy consumption of a cryptocurrency mine with that of a small town.

/imagine A magnifying glass over a dataset, with shadowy figures of people in the background, emphasising the human element in data.

This period also witnessed the rise of the Maker Movement. Platforms like Arduino and Raspberry Pi empowered hobbyists and educators, enabling them to craft custom electronic solutions. From DIY weather stations to home automation systems, creativity was boundless. 3D printing took this a step further, allowing for rapid prototyping and the creation of bespoke physical items. A collage might showcase the diverse array of projects birthed from this movement, emphasising grassroots innovation.

One couldn't discuss the digital symphony without touching upon the deep undertones of cyber warfare. Nations realised that battles of the future might not be fought on physical grounds but in the vast expanses of cyberspace. Stuxnet, a malicious computer worm believed to be a cyberweapon, targeted Iranian nuclear facilities, signalling the dawn of a new warfare age. A timeline could trace major cybersecurity breaches and their global implications.

We see the seeds of quantum computing being sown. Promising capabilities far surpassing classical computers, quantum computing stands poised to be the next major leap, with implications ranging from drug discovery to AI advancements.

In essence, the Digital Symphony is a narrative of contrasts: the tangible versus the virtual, individual creativity versus collective collaboration, rapid progress versus ethical and environmental challenges. Yet, amidst these contrasts, there's harmony, a testament to humanity's unwavering spirit and relentless drive to innovate and evolve. The melodies of the digital age resonate with hope, potential, and a dash of caution, inviting us to both marvel at our achievements and reflect on our responsibilities.

The Spectrum of Intelligence

From the time we began telling stories by the warmth of firelight to the modern age where we explore the furthest reaches of the universe, our understanding of intelligence has shaped our place in the cosmos. The story of intelligence is as old as humanity itself.

When primitive humans first stamped images onto the walls of caves, it was more than an act of mere artistic expression. It was a display of cognitive function, an understanding of symbols, and an ability to communicate complex ideas visually. Consider the first time our ancestors recognised patterns, connecting celestial events like the solstices or equinoxes to changing seasons, crucial for agriculture and survival. This was not just observation but an early form of analytical thinking.

Imagine a vast, detailed mural depicting scenes from our ancient past: tribes collaborating to take down mammoth prey, early scholars charting stars, builders conceptualising pyramids and aqueducts, and philosophers debating in great marble halls. This is the visual journey of human intelligence.

As civilisations rose and fell, our understanding of intelligence evolved. In ancient Greece, intelligence

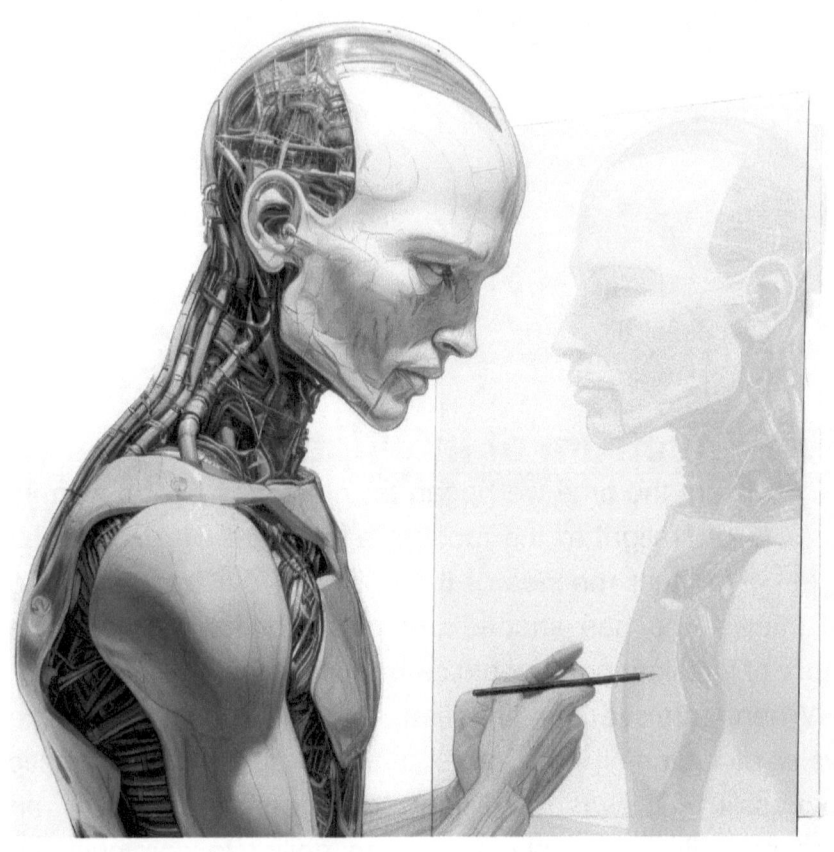

/imagine A humanoid robot looking into a mirror, with its reflection showing lines of code, representing the introspection AI needs.

intertwined with philosophy. Great minds like Plato and Aristotle attempted to understand human thought, linking it to the soul's nature. Their debates formed the bedrock of Western intellectual tradition, setting the stage for future exploration into cognition.

The Renaissance period, a golden age of art, culture, and science, brought fresh perspectives. Thinkers like Leonardo da Vinci exemplified the 'Renaissance Man' ideal – individuals whose expertise spanned a multitude of areas.

Here, intelligence wasn't siloed but celebrated in its diverse manifestations.

Jumping ahead, the 19th and 20th centuries witnessed an explosion in our efforts to quantify and measure intelligence. Psychologists and educators sought standardised metrics, leading to the development of IQ tests. However, as we've learned, intelligence is multifaceted. Dr. Howard Gardner's theory of multiple intelligences shattered the conventional one-size-fits-all approach, proposing that our strengths can range from musical-rhythmic to existential.

Emotional intelligence, too, began to shine as a beacon in the latter half of the 20th century. Its importance in personal relationships, leadership, and overall well-being gave a broader dimension to understanding intelligence.

Parallel to our deepening comprehension of human intelligence was the age-old dream of crafting intelligence. Tales from ancient civilisations spoke of automatons and sentient statues. These myths and legends might be seen as humanity's earliest AI prototypes, embodying our deep-seated desire to recreate ourselves.

The 20th century brought forth technological marvels. Computer systems like IBM's Deep Blue and Watson took on humans in games of chess and Jeopardy and won. These events were watershed moments, signalling that machines could, indeed, mimic certain facets of human cognition.

But the 'intelligence' of these machines was rudimentary, grounded in brute force computational strength rather than nuanced understanding. Enter the era of machine learning. Instead of just being programmed, machines started 'learning', mimicking the neural structures of the human brain.

/imagine Beyond challenges, the future is rife with possibilities. As quantum computing melds with AI, as algorithms become more robust and data more rich, we stand at the precipice of a revolution.

As AI's complexity grew, so did the ethical considerations surrounding it. Philosophers, ethicists, and technologists joined hands in exploring these concerns. How do we define machine rights? What happens when AI makes a decision that harms humans? Who is responsible?

Moreover, as AI began to surpass human capabilities in specific tasks, it raised profound questions about self-worth, identity, and the future of work. If a machine can paint like Picasso, write like Shakespeare, or compose like

Beethoven, what does it mean for human creativity and value?

In sectors like healthcare, the applications of AI offer hope for early diagnosis and personalised treatment. Still, they also carry concerns about privacy, autonomy, and the human touch in care. Imagine a world where your doctor is an AI, offering treatments based on millions of data points. It's efficient, but is it empathetic?

The realm of education, too, stands at AI's frontier. With personalised learning experiences, each student can have a curriculum tailored to their pace and style. But then, what happens to the shared human experience of classrooms, playground dramas, and college friendships?

In this vast spectrum, intelligence, whether biological or artificial, emerges not just as a measure of cognitive prowess but as a tapestry of experiences, emotions, values, and aspirations. As we navigate this landscape, we aren't mere spectators but active participants, shaping, defining, and redefining intelligence's very essence.

There's an acknowledgment: the spectrum of intelligence is vast and ever-evolving. Every development, every discovery, every ethical conundrum adds a new hue, a new tone. And as we look ahead, we recognise that our place in this universe, amidst the grand symphony of stars, galaxies, and the vast unknown, is determined not just by our intelligence but how we choose to wield, celebrate, and nurture it.

If the history of humanity has been a constant quest to understand our surroundings and ourselves, then the heart of this quest lies in our concept of intelligence. Let's delve deeper into the intricate dance between the organic and the inorganic, and the blurring lines in between.

Journey back to ancient civilisations like the Mesopotamians, Egyptians, and the Indus Valley inhabitants. Their monumental architectural achievements, from ziggurats to pyramids, were not only engineering marvels but also symbols of human intelligence and collaboration. The precise measurements, the astronomical alignments, the mathematical rigour – these structures were physical embodiments of human cognition. They were grandiose statements, loud proclamations of our ability to harness intelligence to reshape the natural world.

Zooming in on Egypt, the pyramids weren't just tombs for pharaohs; they were cosmic diagrams, aligning with celestial bodies, showcasing an advanced understanding of the heavens. This celestial mapping, blending the spiritual with the scientific, is a testament to humanity's integrative intelligence, where reason met faith. Such fusions would reappear throughout history, weaving a rich tapestry of intellectual exploration.

The Greeks, with their pantheon of gods and myths, also wove intelligence into their tales. Athena, the goddess of wisdom, symbolised the virtues of strategic warfare and intellect. Oracles, like the one at Delphi, were believed to provide insights into the future – an ancient form of predictive analytics, if you will. In many ways, these oracles served as early prototypes for the predictive algorithms of today's AI systems.

The Middle Ages, often erroneously dubbed the 'Dark Ages', was another crucible of intellectual ferment. Monasteries across Europe preserved ancient texts, ensuring that the knowledge of yore didn't fade into oblivion. Islamic scholars in the Golden Age of Islam translated Greek philosophical works, adding their insights and expanding the realm of mathematics, medicine, and astronomy.

Fast forward to the Enlightenment era. The likes of Kant, Rousseau, and Voltaire challenged existing notions, pushing the boundaries of human thought. Intelligence was no longer just about retaining information; it was about challenging it, dissecting it, and reassembling it in novel ways.

Parallel, in the East, philosophers and scholars from India, China, and Persia were expanding the boundaries of knowledge. Aryabhata, the Indian mathematician, made groundbreaking advances in algebra, while Chinese polymath Shen Kuo documented innovations in astronomy, geology, and engineering.

The Industrial Revolution brought a paradigm shift. Machines started taking over manual tasks, leading to a significant societal reconfiguration. But amidst the cacophony of steam engines and clattering looms, a subtler revolution was underway - the birth of the idea that machines could not just mimic human physicality but also our mentality.

Mathematicians and dreamers like Ada Lovelace and Charles Babbage conceived machines that could compute, laying down the foundations for modern computing. Lovelace, in her annotations, even mused on the idea of machines creating art and music, presciently touching upon the fringes of artificial intelligence.

As the 19th century gave way to the 20th, we see the rise of formal studies into human cognition and psychology. Pioneers like Sigmund Freud and Carl Jung ventured into the human psyche's labyrinthine corridors, exploring the interplay of the conscious and the subconscious. Their work, though centred on the human mind, set the stage for understanding machine 'thinking'. How do machines process information? Can they have a 'subconscious' layer?

The world wars, while largely destructive, inadvertently accelerated technological advancements. Cryptanalysis, signal processing, and operations research – fields that would later underpin AI's development, received significant attention. Post-war, with the advent of the digital age, the pace was relentless. Computers shrunk from room-sized behemoths to desktop companions, and then to devices that fit in our pockets. With this miniaturisation came an exponential growth in computational power.

As we edge closer to our times, AI's manifestations are everywhere, from the algorithms recommending movies on streaming platforms to advanced robotics in manufacturing units. But with these advances, society grapples with essential questions about identity, agency, ethics, and purpose.

The vast panorama of intelligence's history, stretching from ancient civilisations to the digital age, underscores a fundamental truth: intelligence is not static. It's a dynamic force, evolving, adapting, and transforming. It is an interplay of biology and environment, of nature and nurture, of organic neurones and silicon circuits.

We stand at a crossroads. Behind us is the winding path of discovery and understanding, marked by milestones of human and machine intelligence. Ahead lies an uncharted territory, a horizon filled with possibilities and pitfalls. How we navigate this terrain, harnessing the combined might of human insight and machine precision, will determine our shared future. A future where the spectrum of intelligence shines brightly, illuminating our path.

Learning curve

Every epoch in human history has a tale to tell. Ours is sung to the rhythm of electrons and pixels, a poetic blend of organic wonder and artificial prowess. As the narrative continues to unfold, a finer understanding of today's defining technologies is essential.

At the heart of modern artificial intelligence lies a profound structure known as the neural network. While its nomenclature is borrowed from biology—the vast web of neurons that constitute the human brain—its implementation is purely digital. However, the parallels between these two systems provide a captivating starting point for our exploration.

Imagine the brain, an organ with over a hundred billion neurons, each forming thousands of connections to its counterparts, resulting in a system of unparalleled complexity. The digital counterpart, while not yet matching the organic brain's vastness, attempts to emulate its functionality. Each node in a neural network acts as a neuron, transmitting and processing data, learning, adapting, and evolving.

The concept of 'learning' in these networks is a marvel in itself. Much as a child learns to differentiate between shapes, colours, or sounds, a neural network hones its understanding through repeated exposure to data. For example, by processing thousands of images of cats, it learns the distinguishing features: whiskers, tails, feline eyes. Over time, and with consistent training, it can reliably identify a cat in a new, unseen image.

This iterative training process bears striking resemblance to human learning patterns. If a neural network's prediction is incorrect, the error is computed and fed back into the system. The connections, or weights, between nodes are adjusted. Over time, these minute adjustments, accumulated and compounded, lead to a refined, accurate network. The beauty lies in the simplicity of the individual operations and the complexity arising from their collective execution.

Deep learning—a term that sounds both mysterious and profound—is essentially a progression of the neural network concept. If you visualise a neural network as a shallow pond, deep learning is the vast, fathomless ocean.

The 'depth' in deep learning refers to the multiple layers in these neural networks. Each layer captures different features. In the context of image recognition, initial layers might detect edges, the subsequent ones recognise shapes formed by these edges, further layers identify complex structures like eyes or noses, and the final layers could recognise the entire object—a face, an animal, or any other entity.

But the applications of deep learning extend beyond image recognition. Think of voice assistants. When you ask Siri or Alexa a question, deep learning algorithms process your voice, understand the query's context, and respond.

These systems have been fed vast amounts of data—varied accents, languages, and nuances—and trained to understand and respond. This depth of learning enables natural, smooth interactions with machines, a feat that seemed like science fiction just decades ago.

Quantum computing, a term that's been buzzing in scientific circles, promises to redefine our understanding of computation. Traditional computers use bits—binary units that can be either 0s or 1s. Quantum computers use qubits, units that leverage quantum mechanics properties, enabling them to be in a state of superposition. This means they can be 0, 1, or both simultaneously.

But why is this revolutionary? Think of a massive maze. A classical computer would attempt each path sequentially, searching for the exit. A quantum computer, however, could explore multiple routes simultaneously. Problems that would take classical computers billions of years could potentially be solved by quantum computers in seconds.

Beyond superposition, another quantum principle, entanglement, plays a role. If two qubits become entangled, the state of one qubit will instantly influence the other, regardless of the distance separating them. This profound connection further augments the computational power of quantum systems.

The narrative would be incomplete without appreciating today's advancements in visualisation and interaction. 3D holography, once limited to the realms of sci-fi, is now a tangible reality. These aren't mere projections; they are interactive, dynamic, and incredibly detailed.

Imagine attending a medical lecture. Instead of 2D slides, a 3D holographic human heart hovers before you, beating, showcasing its chambers, valves, and veins. You can zoom in, rotate, or even dissect it with hand gestures. This immersive experience transforms learning, making it interactive and engaging.

Similarly, architectural models can be visualised in full 3D, exploring every nook and corner, every planned tree in the garden, or the intricate patterns on a proposed facade. The realm of design, education, entertainment, and more are undergoing radical transformations thanks to these visualisation technologies.

The rhythms of today echo the innovations of AI, the depths of machine learning, and the enigmatic dances of quantum realms. Every online purchase recommendation, every voice-activated command, every secured transaction, and even every tagged photo on social media platforms is a testament to the intricate dance of algorithms behind the scenes.

However, this isn't just a dance of machines. It's a dance of humanity intertwined with its creations. Every programmer, data scientist, engineer, and visionary contributes steps to this dance. As AI systems diagnose diseases, predict weather patterns, or even craft art, they reflect the collective aspirations of countless individuals who've contributed to this domain.

One realises that today's dance is a mesmerising blend of art and science, tradition and innovation, challenges and solutions. While the leaps in AI and technology are phenomenal, they also bear the weight of responsibility. The path forward isn't just about pushing boundaries but ensuring these advancements benefit all of humanity, fostering a brighter, more inclusive future.

A dance is remembered not just for its grand leaps but also for its subtle moves. Similarly, the charm of today's technological marvels isn't just in the groundbreaking innovations but in how seamlessly they've woven themselves into the fabric of our daily lives.

So what are the real examples? Lets start with the Smart Home. The concept of a 'smart home' has rapidly transitioned from being a luxurious novelty to an almost essential modern convenience. The conveniences range from refrigerators that suggest recipes based on their contents, to thermostats that learn your preferences over time and adjust the heating or cooling autonomously. But beyond convenience, they offer enhanced safety – security cameras with facial recognition, doorbells that notify homeowners of familiar or unfamiliar visitors, and smoke alarms that can pinpoint the exact location of a fire.

Imagine waking up to the scent of brewed coffee, your home already having adjusted the ambient temperature to your preference, and as you enter your workspace, the lights adjust based on the outside lighting. This isn't the plot of a futuristic movie. This is today.

Also, the Era of Virtual Personal Assistants growing. Alexa, Siri, Cortana, and Google Assistant: names that have almost become family members in many households. These virtual assistants, with their deep learning capacities, cater to our commands and queries. From setting alarms to reciting recipes, updating us about weather conditions to playing our favourite tunes, they've added a rhythm to our routines.

What's remarkable is their ability to understand context. Ask about the weather, and they might suggest taking an umbrella if rain is predicted. If you're asking about a recipe, they might also offer to set a timer for cooking. This contextual understanding, achieved through extensive neural

With each picture shown, the child (or in our case, the machine) gets better at identifying the animal

/imagine the child (or in our case, the machine) gets better at identifying the animal

network training, makes interactions feel less robotic and more organic.

Even more, we are heading to revolution in healthcare. Today's dance doesn't just entertain; it heals. AI's intersection with healthcare is creating wonders. Wearable tech like smartwatches can now detect irregular heart rhythms or falls and can even initiate emergency responses.

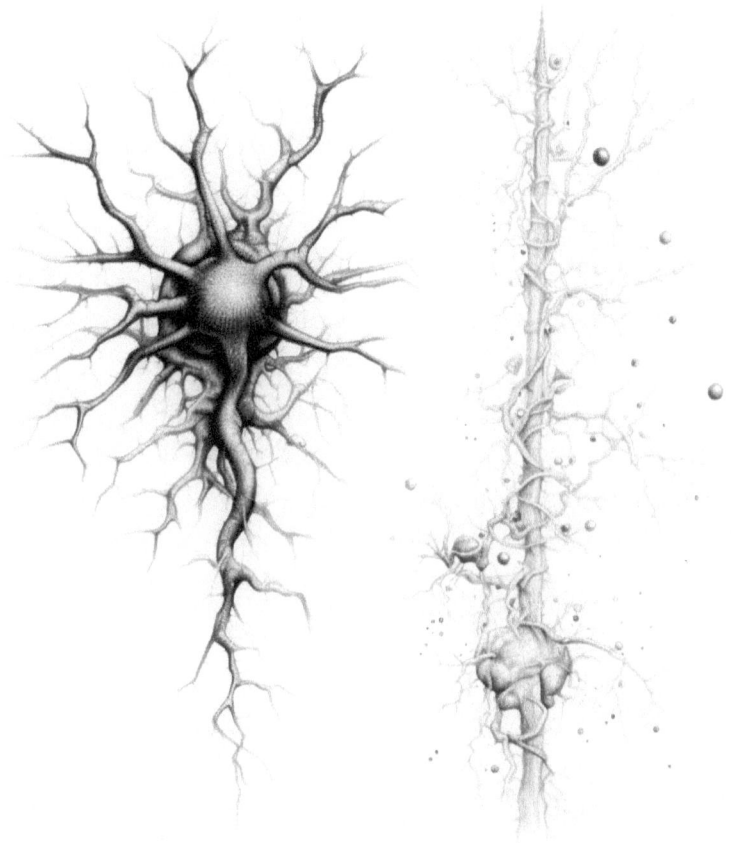

/imagine A side-by-side comparison of a biological neuron with dendrites and synapses and an artificial neuron with weighted inputs and an activation function.

Imagine the boon for elderly individuals, granting them a measure of independence and their loved ones a sense of security.

Machine learning models are assisting radiologists in spotting tumours in X-rays and MRIs with increased accuracy. In many instances, these models have identified anomalies that were missed by the human eye. Their ability to cross-reference vast amounts of data means they can provide more accurate diagnoses, revolutionising patient care.

And it's not just about diagnostics. AI-powered robots have been assisting surgeons, enabling precision that reduces operative risks. Virtual consultations, especially significant in the age of remote everything, ensure medical assistance even in the remotest of areas.

If individual homes have become smarter, can entire cities be far behind? The concept of smart cities goes beyond mere automation; it's about optimisation. AI algorithms process data from a myriad of sensors scattered across the city to optimise traffic flows, reduce energy consumption, monitor environmental factors, and provide real-time data to city administrators for improved governance.

Waste management becomes efficient as sensors in bins notify when they're full. Traffic lights adjust in real time to prevent congestion. Surveillance systems equipped with AI ensure safety and help in immediate crisis response. Every element of the city communicates, ensuring a harmonious living experience for its inhabitants.

Many fear that AI might stifle creativity. But, the reality is far from it. Artists are using AI to push the boundaries of creativity. There are AI algorithms that can craft music, paint portraits, or write poetry. These aren't mere imitations but unique creations.

Consider the realm of filmmaking. AI can assist in editing, choosing shots based on the emotional tone set by the director. They can suggest soundtracks, enhance visual effects, or even predict audience reactions to certain sequences.

In concluding this extended look into our present, one cannot help but be awed. Today's technological tapestry is rich, varied, and constantly evolving. Yet, at its core, it mirrors human aspirations and dreams. AI isn't an alien entity; it's a reflection of our collective consciousness, an ode to human curiosity, and a tool for progress.

Each thread of this narrative, whether it's the smart device in our hands, the virtual worlds we explore, or the quantum computations we're just beginning to fathom, is an integral part of the mosaic of modern life. The promise isn't just of a smarter world but of one that's more connected, empathetic, and harmonious. The future holds immense promise, but it's rooted in the steps we take today.

Bridging the Digital Realm

The heart of today's technological age beats to a rhythm defined by the intricate dance of algorithms, vast neural networks, and the seemingly mystical realm of quantum mechanics. This chapter will guide the reader through a vivid journey of the marvels of the digital age.

Neural networks, at their core, are inspired by the complex web of neurons that make up our brains. Each neuron in this digital structure takes in data, processes it, and passes it on — not unlike the way our biological neurons function.

Delving deeper, imagine walking through a vast forest. Each tree represents a neuron, and the leaves are the interconnected dendrites. Data, like sunlight, filters through these leaves, nourishing the tree and enabling it to grow. As more data streams in, the forest becomes denser, and the trees' roots intertwine and deepen. This is akin to how a neural network learns, adapting and evolving with each new piece of information.

Such networks enable machines to recognise patterns, learn from data, and make predictions. The result? Facial recognition that tags us in photos, voice assistants that understand our commands, and self-driving cars that navigate our roads.

A subset of machine learning, deep learning, is like taking the aforementioned forest and placing it in layers, each more intricate and specialised than the last. As data flows, each layer processes and refines the information. The first layer might simply recognise edges and corners. The subsequent ones would identify shapes, then textures, and so on until the final layer discerns, for instance, a human face.

Deep learning has fostered breakthroughs in numerous fields. Medical diagnostics, for instance, benefit from algorithms that can identify potential tumours with astonishing precision. In the realm of entertainment, it's the magic behind realistic video game graphics and the eerily lifelike movements of CGI characters in films.

Enter the enigmatic world of quantum computing, where bits are replaced by qubits and the laws of physics as we know them are beautifully, bizarrely, defied. Traditional computers see bits as either 0s or 1s. Qubits, however, harness the power of quantum superposition, existing in a state that is both 0 and 1 simultaneously.

Imagine standing at a vast library's entrance. A traditional computer would read each book one by one to find a specific piece of information. A quantum computer, in contrast, would scan all books simultaneously, drawing the desired data in mere moments.

While quantum computing is still in its nascent stages, its potential is staggering. From revolutionising drug discovery by simulating complex molecular structures to enhancing AI capabilities, the future it promises is vibrant.

3D holographic images emerge, transporting readers right into the heart of these innovations. Drones, equipped with advanced AI, hover gracefully above meticulously designed smart cities, their cameras capturing every movement, ensuring safety, and optimising traffic flows.

A leap into a modern hospital showcases virtual doctors — avatars powered by advanced AI algorithms. They consult with patients, analyse symptoms, and even assist human doctors during surgeries, their precision and speed enhanced by the power of deep learning.

Despite the breathtaking pace of advancement, at the heart of every algorithm, every neural network, and every quantum computer, lies humanity's innate curiosity and desire to push boundaries. Each innovation is not just a testament to our intellectual prowess but also a tool to enhance our quality of life.

To conclude, as the world dances to the tune of today's technological marvels, one thing remains clear: the harmonious blend of technology and humanity is not just shaping our present but also carving pathways into the future.

The journey of understanding is far from over. As we stand at this pivotal point in history, it is crucial to embrace these advancements, understand their implications, and navigate the future with knowledge and empathy.

Beyond the immediate tangible realities, our world has started to blur the lines between the digital and the physical. Augmented reality (AR) and virtual reality (VR) stand at this fascinating intersection.

Augmented Reality: Here, digital information — be it images, sounds, or other data — overlays physical space. Picture walking down a historical street and, through AR glasses, witnessing reconstructions of events from centuries ago. Museums come alive as artefacts narrate their own stories. Even mundane activities, like shopping, transform. Envision trying on clothes virtually, with your AR device suggesting styles based on your preferences and body type.

Virtual Reality: Stepping further from the tangible, VR immerses users in entirely digital realms. Here, realities are crafted from scratch, limited only by imagination. The applications are vast. Architects walk clients through buildings not yet built; therapists treat phobias by gradually exposing patients to their fears in controlled virtual environments; and educators take students on journeys through time or even within the human body.

As we weave through this digital tapestry, holograms project these realities, making them palpable. Through 3D visualisations, we can almost touch the digital artefacts, feel the pulse of virtual worlds, and sense the melding of the real and the virtual.

Amid the auditory experiences that today's tech offers, Natural Language Processing (NLP) stands out. This technology powers our conversations with virtual assistants, our text predictions, and even translates languages in real-time.

Dive into its intricacies, and one realises NLP isn't just about understanding words but deciphering context, tone, and intent. It's a dance of syntax, semantics, and sentiment. With deep learning models, machines today can grasp sarcasm, detect mood shifts in texts, and even craft poetry.

The written word gains dimension with visuals of intricate neural pathways lighting up as they process languages. Diagrams trace the journey from basic word recognition to complex context comprehension. The dance of algorithms in this realm is poetic, almost mirroring the rhythm of human conversation.

As cities grow smarter and machines more sentient, there's an ever-present concern about our planet's well-being. Fortunately, AI has been a beacon of hope here too. Drones, powered by AI, monitor vast forest areas, detecting early signs of wildfires or illegal logging activities. Advanced algorithms analyse climate data, offering predictions and insights that could be pivotal for our survival.

Through stunning visuals, readers witness the lush green expanse of forests monitored by drones, the vast blue oceans with AI-powered equipment tracking marine health, and the urban landscapes where AI assists in optimising resource consumption.

In an increasingly connected world, security is paramount. With every advancement comes the looming threat of cyberattacks. Enter AI-driven cybersecurity. Through machine learning, systems detect unusual patterns, flagging potential threats. Quantum encryption methods emerge as the new guardians of data, promising unparalleled security.

Graphical representations provide a bird's-eye view of digital landscapes, dotted with firewalls and protective algorithms, weaving a protective web around our data. It's a vivid portrayal of the digital fortress that safeguards our interconnected lives.

From smart homes, we've moved to smart lifestyles. Today, AI-driven algorithms suggest what we eat, wear, and even whom we date. The luxury industry has been particularly transformed. Imagine a virtual stylist powered by AI, which understands your preferences, current fashion trends, and even the occasion you're dressing for, offering tailor-made suggestions.

Lavish illustrations showcase AI-powered luxury — be it in fashion, gourmet dining, or travel. The images resonate with opulence, yet there's an underlying theme of personalisation, of AI understanding individual tastes and preferences.

One cannot help but marvel at the intricate choreography of today's tech-driven world. It's a ballet of bits and qubits, a harmonious melding of past innovations and future possibilities.

Our journey has been long, from understanding the very genesis of our digital age to witnessing its current grandeur. The dance floor is vast, and the dance continues, ever-evolving, promising a future that's not just smarter but also more humane, compassionate, and inclusive.

Ethical Crossroads

The development and evolution of AI is a testament to human ingenuity, but it's not a journey without its crossroads. These intersections force society to consider not only technological feasibility but also moral and ethical responsibility. As AI becomes a dominant force in our daily lives, the quandaries it poses become ever more intricate and pressing.

To understand the challenges posed by AI, it's necessary first to grasp its underlying mechanics. Much of AI's learning is based on vast datasets fed into algorithms, which are essentially patterns and rules the system follows to make decisions. When these datasets carry inherent biases or inaccuracies, the AI system perpetuates and even magnifies those biases.

Consider an illustration of a scale, teetering precariously. On one side are vast heaps of data, representing all the information AI systems have been trained on, and on the other, a perfect, unbiased decision, still unachieved. This balance is hard to strike.

Real-world Mishaps and Lessons Learned

/imagine A layered depiction of a neural network, each layer intricately connected, showing how data flows and is processed

1. The Judicial Misstep: One of the most infamous misapplications of AI has been in the criminal justice system. In certain countries, predictive policing algorithms forecast where crimes might occur and who might commit them. However, these algorithms were found to be biased against certain racial groups, leading to unwarranted arrests and perpetuating stereotypes. Here, a sketch could show a darkened city, with spotlight beams, representing AI predictions, disproportionately focusing on specific neighbourhoods.

2. Biased Hiring Practices: AI-driven recruitment tools promised efficiency. Yet, when trained on historical hiring data, some of these systems developed a preference for male candidates over female candidates for certain job roles.

3. The Sentiment Analysis Flaw: Sentiment analysis algorithms, designed to gauge public opinion on social media, have often misinterpreted neutral statements from certain dialects or languages as negative, highlighting the danger of a one-size-fits-all approach. Visualise a globe, with different regions emitting signals, some mistakenly marked in red.

The Philosophical Quandaries

1. The Trolley Problem Reimagined for AI: This classical ethical dilemma gains new dimensions with autonomous vehicles. Should a self-driving car, to avoid hitting several pedestrians, swerve and risk the life of its passenger? This vivid illustration could juxtapose the traditional trolley tracks with a modern city street, the choices stark and challenging.

2. Determining AI Rights: As AI systems grow more advanced, can they possess rights? If an AI system can create art, who owns the copyright? A sketch might show an AI unit, brushes in mechanical arms, painting a masterpiece, while in the shadows, figures debate ownership.

3. The Ethics of AI in Warfare: Drones and automated weaponry have changed the face of warfare. But who bears responsibility when AI-led missions cause collateral damage? An illustration here could be haunting: a juxtaposition of a remote AI control room and a devastated battlefield.

Utopian Dreams and Dystopian Nightmares

71

1. The Utopian Vision: A world where AI aids humanity in every conceivable way. Pollution is curbed with AI monitoring and managing waste. Education becomes personalised, with AI tutors catering to each student's needs. Healthcare, too, is revolutionised, with AI predicting potential health issues before they become severe.

2. The Dystopian Fear: On the flip side, the unchecked growth of AI could lead to pervasive surveillance. Personal privacy could be eroded, with every action, online or offline, monitored and analysed. Employment crises could ensue as AI systems replace human jobs, leading to socio-economic disparities. This grim future might be visualised as a grey, Orwellian world, with towering screens monitoring citizens and drones hovering, casting ominous shadows.

It's evident that AI, for all its brilliance, is a mirror reflecting the best and worst of humanity. Its ethical implementation is not just the responsibility of technologists but of society at large.

Ensuring ethical AI requires diverse teams that can recognise and rectify biases. Regulations and guidelines, both national and international, need to be instituted to ensure fairness and transparency.

A maze illustration, alluded to earlier, finds its place here. We trace paths, symbolising various ethical decisions, some leading to dead ends, others to clearer roads, embodying the challenges and decisions society faces.

In conclusion, while AI promises a future of unparalleled advancement, it also presents profound ethical dilemmas. The dance between technology and morality is intricate, and humanity's choices in the coming years will dictate whether AI remains a boon or manifests as a tool of inadvertent bias and control. The song of the future is ours to compose, and every note, every beat, matters.

One of the foundational pillars upon which AI is constructed is data. Without data, AI remains an empty shell, a potential left unfulfilled. But what happens when the data is skewed or tainted with prejudice?

One might think of data as just numbers, void of emotion or motive. However, data is a snapshot of societal trends, behaviours, and choices. When the society from which this data is drawn is inherently biased, the data reflects those biases. An illustration here could depict a river, labeled "Data Stream," drawing from various societal sources. If these sources are polluted with prejudice, the river carries those impurities downstream.

Beyond just theoretical discussions, biased data has real-world implications. Whether it's minorities being profiled because training data lacked their fair representation or voice recognition software struggling with certain accents due to predominantly Western-centric training, the ramifications are manifold and widespread.

Addressing this issue requires a concerted effort. Strategies involve using balanced datasets, penalising models that display bias, and third-party audits of AI algorithms. Imagine a graphic with various AI professionals working diligently, filtering data, adjusting algorithms, and ensuring fairness in AI operations.

The realms of AI capabilities are vast, and as we advance, a pertinent question arises: Can AI feel? Does it have emotions, or is it merely mimicking patterns it's been trained upon?

Emulating Emotion: Currently, AI models, like chatbots, can "emulate" emotion. They can recognise human emotions based on text inputs or facial recognition and respond accordingly. However, this recognition and response are based on learned patterns, not genuine feelings. A side-by-side illustration might show a human brain with its intricate neural connections juxtaposed against an AI neural network, illustrating the difference yet similarity.

The Sentience Debate: Philosophers and AI experts alike grapple with this. If an AI system were to achieve consciousness, would it have rights? Would shutting down such a system be considered a moral violation? Visual depictions of various scholars in animated debate can be peppered throughout this section, highlighting its controversial nature.

One of the most tangible and immediate impacts of AI is its disruption of the job market. Automation and AI-driven processes have brought efficiency but have also rendered certain jobs obsolete.

A Historical Perspective: Every technological revolution, from the Industrial Age to the Information Age, has seen a shift in job dynamics. A timeline illustration here can depict the major technological eras and corresponding job shifts.

While roles like data entry or basic customer support might diminish, new roles are emerging, such as AI ethicists or AI trainers. However, the transition isn't always smooth. A graphic of a seesaw, on one side "Jobs Lost" and the other "Jobs Created," teetering, aptly captures this dynamic.

As the old adage goes, "When one door closes, another opens." In the face of AI-driven changes, the emphasis on reskilling and retraining cannot be understated. Lifelong learning becomes paramount. A picturesque graphic showing individuals of various ages, from young to old, all engaged in learning, underlines this message.

Rather than viewing AI as a competitor, a more constructive perspective is to see it as a collaborator. This section delves into the beautiful symphony of human-AI collaboration.

Humans have intuition, emotions, creativity, and morals. AI possesses speed, accuracy, and vast data processing capabilities. When combined, the potential is astronomical. Visuals here might depict humans and AI, not in opposition, but hand in hand, climbing a mountain symbolising progress.

Healthcare Miracles: AI-driven diagnostics combined with human doctors' expertise results in improved patient outcomes. In complex surgeries, precision robotics, guided by human hands, ensure unparalleled accuracy. Illustrative snapshots could capture these collaborative moments in healthcare settings.

Art and AI: AI is not just about cold, hard logic. It's venturing into the domain of art, creating music, paintings, and literature. But rather than replacing human artists, it's amplifying their capabilities. Vivid images of AI systems and humans jointly engaged in artistic endeavours can punctuate this section.

The ethical crossroads presented by AI is not just a technological issue but a deeply human one. Decisions made today will echo for generations to come. We will close the chapter with an open question, urging you to engage actively with these issues, ensuring that AI's journey ahead is aligned with human values and aspirations.

Peppered throughout are interactive elements, quizzes, thought experiments, and real-life case studies, ensuring readers don't just passively consume content but actively engage with the profound questions posed.

Tomorrow's Horizon

As the first rays of dawn cast a warm, golden hue across the horizon, humanity stands on the precipice of a future intertwined with artificial intelligence. In this dreamscape, we aren't bound by the limitations of our current understanding but are propelled by the sheer vastness of what might be. This is the realm of projections, dreams, speculations, and profound what-ifs.

The Enigmatic Evolution: Just as stars sparkle in the vast expanse of our universe, so does the potential evolution of AI in our near and distant futures. A magnificent, fold-out star chart beckons readers, encouraging them to trace possible trajectories of AI. From its current state as a tool and companion, could it evolve into a sentient being, with desires, dreams, and dilemmas of its own? Or might it merge with human consciousness, leading to a harmonious symbiosis, a blend of organic and artificial like never before witnessed?

A cloud of luminous points on the star chart represents varied potentialities. Some are bright and close, indicating imminent advancements, while others, more dim and distant, symbolise the profound and far-reaching. Yet, each glimmering point holds a story, a potential future where AI plays a pivotal role.

Ethereal illustrations immerse readers in landscapes where cities float, where humans and AI entities co-create art, and where interstellar travel is not just possible but an everyday event, thanks to the immense computational capacities of evolved AI. But, it's not just utopias that this horizon holds. Darker visions emerge—of surveillance states where privacy is a myth, of AI entities rebelling against their

creators, and of societies where the human touch is lost, replaced by cold, mechanical interactions.

A vivid illustration portrays this duality: one half bathed in golden light, showing harmonious scenes of man and machine, while the other half, shaded in cooler blues and grays, delves into the challenges and potential perils.

More than ever, it becomes evident that the trajectory AI takes isn't just about its programming. It's about the hopes, fears, ambitions, and ethics of its creators—us. It's about decisions made in boardrooms, in research labs, in political arenas, and even in our homes. Every choice, every ethical stance, and every dream contributes to the rhythm to which AI dances.

Gazing into the future also brings with it a weight of responsibility. With the immense potential AI holds, comes the duty to ensure that its development and deployment are done with care, consideration, and a deep respect for all of humanity. Animated illustrations depict potential scenarios: An AI-driven medical breakthrough saving lives, juxtaposed against a biased AI system causing societal discord.

What kind of future do they envision? How can they contribute to a harmonious evolution of AI? The ethereal illustrations, which have been their companions throughout this visionary journey, morph into blank canvases, encouraging readers to sketch, dream, and envision their own horizons.

The narrative doesn't just end—it echoes, leaving a lasting resonance. The responsibility doesn't conclude with understanding; it just begins. For in the hands of an enlightened society, AI isn't just a tool—it's a beacon, guiding us toward a future of our own creation.

We are enveloped in a whirlwind of emotions: Awe at the vastness of possibilities, caution borne from understanding potential pitfalls, and an invigorating sense of responsibility.

They aren't just equipped with knowledge but also with a vision, a dream, and a fervent hope for a tomorrow where AI and humanity stride forth, hand in hand, towards horizons yet unseen.

Tomorrow's horizon is not solely built upon the imaginations of today, but also upon the aspirations of yesteryears. Legends of the past dreamt of flying machines, of communications that transcended vast distances in mere moments, of elixirs that could heal any ailment. Today, we see glimmers of these dreams coming true, in part due to the marvels of AI. But who are the pioneers charting this new course?

Dive deep into the stories of these innovators. Some are names recognised globally—scientists, entrepreneurs, thinkers. Others are unsung heroes—students in dorm rooms, engineers in bustling tech hubs, philosophers in contemplative retreats. Their collective ambition doesn't just add, it multiplies, amplifying the potential for what AI can achieve.

Each profile, each story, not only showcases their achievements but also their dreams. How does a teenager in Seoul imagine AI transforming education? What does a senior researcher in Nairobi envision for AI in agriculture in the next two decades? These individual hopes and anticipations coalesce to form a mosaic of potential futures.

The march into the future is not a solitary journey. It's a collective dance of cultures, histories, and traditions. As AI integrates more into the societal fabric, it inevitably intertwines with cultural nuances. Imagine an AI deeply rooted in the philosophies of Ubuntu, emphasising communal values and collective harmony. Or consider an AI

/imagine A balance scale, on one side, an intricate, detailed model representing overfitting, and on the other, a crude, simplistic model depicting underfitting

system based on the principles of 'Wabi-sabi', finding beauty in imperfection and transience.

These AIs interacting in various cultural festivals—Diwali, Hanami, Carnival. They learn, adapt, and even celebrate. In this dance, AI doesn't just assimilate; it enhances, enriching the tapestry of global traditions with its unique insights and capabilities.

One of the profound capabilities of advanced AI is the creation and exploration of virtual worlds. Tomorrow's horizon may not just be about our physical realm but also these ethereal landscapes. Detailed illustrations immerse readers into these dimensions—some surreal with floating islands and phosphorescent forests, others mirroring our own with such precision it's hard to distinguish reality from replication.

Within these realms, the line between creator and inhabitant blurs. An AI might design a realm based on its understanding of human nostalgia, while another might craft a sanctuary reflecting its interpretation of peace. The interplay between AI-created and human-inhabited spaces could redefine experiences, memories, and perhaps even consciousness.

Ripples in the Economic Waters: As AI evolves, so do economies. Predictions about job markets, financial systems, and global trade are intricately illustrated. An AI-driven agrarian revolution optimising yields, a decentralised blockchain AI managing real-time global trades, or virtual architects crafting digital realms. However, alongside these positive projections are more sobering ones. Job displacements, economic disparities, the dichotomy of abundance and want. Addressing these requires not just technological solutions but ethical, societal, and political will.

Interstellar Ideations: Tomorrow's horizon may stretch beyond our blue planet. With advancements in AI-driven space exploration, the dream of interstellar colonisation and cosmic discovery beckons. Flowing illustrations show AI-powered spacecraft navigating nebulae, robotic-AI hybrids mining asteroids, and deep-space AI observatories unraveling cosmic mysteries. Yet, the question lingers: As we venture out, what version of humanity, aided by AI, do we take to the stars?

Philosophical Paradigms and AI: As AI progresses, it doesn't just challenge technological thresholds but also philosophical ones. What does it mean to be sentient? Can an AI ever attain a state of 'enlightenment'? Dialogues between AI and human philosophers, intricately penned, pose profound questions and explore potential answers.

Every bit of progress, every leap into the unknown brings with it choices. Choices that determine not just the role of AI in our future but the very essence of what that future looks like. A future crafted with wisdom, foresight, and a sense of shared destiny can ensure that the horizon we march towards is one of hope, harmony, and holistic growth.

PART 2

Deciphering the AI Enigma

The Mechanics of Thought - Unraveling AI

As we embark on this journey into the labyrinth of artificial intelligence, it's imperative to understand its heartbeat, the mechanics that fuel its prowess. Just as a musical maestro crafts symphonies from individual notes, the AI weaves its magic from data and algorithms.

At its core, AI is about data. Imagine data as the raw clay that an artist uses. The quality, consistency, and attributes of this clay dictate the final artwork. In a similar vein, the data fed into an AI system influences its outputs.

In the world of AI, data can come in many flavours.

Structured Data: Think spreadsheets. Rows, columns, identifiable patterns. Examples include databases storing product prices or customer details.

Unstructured Data: This is more chaotic. Pictures, videos, random text. An example would be social media posts or YouTube videos.

From Data to Information: The next step involves distilling raw data into usable information. This is akin to the artist choosing the right mix of clay, moulding it, and preparing it

/imagine A visual representation showing the progression from raw, unorganised data to clean, structured information.

for the masterpiece. This process involves data cleaning, normalisation, and transformation.

The essence of AI lies in its ability to learn. But how does a machine learn? Machine Learning (ML) is the answer. At its heart, ML is about teaching computers to recognise patterns and make decisions based on data without explicit programming.

For instance, let's consider a simple machine learning task: Identifying whether a given picture is of a cat or not. The machine initially knows nothing about cats. But as it's exposed to pictures (data), some labeled 'cat' and others labeled 'not cat', it starts recognising patterns—whiskers, feline eyes, tails. Eventually, when presented with a new image, the machine can confidently say, "This is a cat" or "This isn't a cat".

Just as architects rely on blueprints to construct buildings, ML relies on algorithms. Algorithms are sets of rules or processes that the machine follows in its learning phase.

Example: Let's dive into a straightforward algorithm - the Decision Tree. Imagine you're trying to decide if you should carry an umbrella. Your decision might be based on factors like the likelihood of rain, the presence of dark clouds, or the humidity level. A decision tree would systematically evaluate each factor to arrive at a conclusion.

As AI has evolved, so have the algorithms. Today, we have neural networks, deep learning models, and reinforcement learning, which are inspired by human brains, allowing machines to process vast amounts of data and recognise complex patterns.

ML involves two critical phases—training and testing. Consider the analogy of a student studying for an exam. The student reads, revises, and understands various subjects during the training phase. Come exam time (testing phase), the student's knowledge is evaluated.

Similarly, in ML, during the training phase, the machine is exposed to a vast dataset, learning patterns and making associations. Once trained, it's tested on a new set of data to verify its accuracy and reliability.

AI, with all its brilliance, is not infallible. There are challenges like overfitting (where the model is too narrowly trained and performs poorly on new data) and under-fitting (where the model is too generalised and lacks accuracy).

Furthermore, it's essential to recognise that AI doesn't "think" like humans. It doesn't have emotions, consciousness, or intuition. It operates based on data and learned patterns.

As this chapter concludes, we recognise AI as both an art and science. It's an amalgamation of data, algorithms, training, and continuous learning. But beyond the mechanics, AI's magic lies in its applications, its potential to transform realms, which we will continue to explore in subsequent chapters.

As we tread deeper into the realms of artificial intelligence, the maze of its workings comes into sharper focus. AI, a field that promises revolutionary advances, is fundamentally rooted in the confluence of data, algorithms, and computational prowess.

In the vast universe of AI, if algorithms are the stars, data is the cosmic matter that binds them. Data provides context, substance, and the foundational material upon which algorithms operate.

Data doesn't appear out of thin air. It's meticulously collected from various sources—sensors, user inputs, digital platforms, and more. Every click online, every digital transaction, every GPS location tag—these are potential data points.

But collection isn't straightforward. There are challenges like privacy concerns, noise in data, and ensuring a diverse and representative sample. Collecting data is as much about ethics and responsibility as it is about technology. The quality of data determines the quality of AI outputs. Outliers, missing values, duplicates—these can skew results. Thus, data cleaning becomes paramount.

While data is the fuel, machine learning is the engine that powers AI. It's the process that allows computers to improve from experience.

Not all learning is the same. Depending on the nature of data and the problem at hand, different approaches are employed:

Supervised Learning: Here, the algorithm is trained on a labeled dataset. Think of it as a teacher supervising a student. The algorithm predicts outputs based on inputs, and any error is corrected using the provided labels.

Example: An email spam filter. The algorithm is trained using emails labeled as 'spam' or 'not spam'. Once trained, it can classify new emails into these categories.

Unsupervised Learning: No labels are provided here. The algorithm tries to understand and uncover patterns in the data on its own.

Example: Customer segmentation. Here, an algorithm can cluster similar customers based on purchasing behavior without knowing any predefined categories.

Reinforcement Learning: This is about trial and error. An agent takes actions in an environment to maximise cumulative reward.

Example: Training a robot to navigate a maze. The robot

/imagine A triptych of scenes: a classroom (supervised), an explorer in a jungle (unsupervised), and a gamer navigating challenges (reinforcement).

earns a reward for finding the exit and penalties for hitting walls.

Algorithms, in essence, are sets of rules or procedures for solving problems. They dictate how data is processed, patterns recognised, and decisions made.

As AI's horizon expands, so does the repertoire of algorithms. From support vector machines to genetic algorithms, the toolkit is vast and varied.

Bridging the chasm between traditional machine learning and human-like AI is the realm of neural networks and deep learning.

Inspired by biological neurons, an artificial neuron receives inputs, processes them, and produces an output. Multiple neurons connected form a neural network.

When neural networks have many layers, allowing for complex pattern recognition, it's termed as deep learning. From voice assistants understanding natural language to software identifying potential tumours in X-rays, deep learning is behind many AI marvels.

Traditional computers, powerful as they are, have limitations. Enter quantum computing—a realm where bits (the smallest data units in classical computing) are replaced by quantum bits or qubits.

Quantum computers promise exponentially faster processing speeds, paving the way for complex problem-solving, be it drug discovery or optimising vast supply chains.

While the progress in AI is dazzling, challenges abound. Issues of bias, interpretability, and generalisation are critical. The tools we design inherit our imperfections, and there's a constant endeavour to refine, understand, and control them better.

AI isn't just a tool—it's a testament to human ingenuity and an embodiment of our aspirations. The world of Artificial Intelligence is one of meticulous crafting and transformation. Much like an artist chisels away at a block of marble to reveal the masterpiece within, AI developers, through the processes of training and inference and with the help of vast amounts of data, sculpt intelligence out of raw computational resources.

Imagine a child, curious and eager, stepping into the world for the first time. Every experience, every lesson, and every interaction shapes their understanding, moulding their cognitive faculties. This formative process, in the realm of AI, is known as training.

Training is an iterative process where a model learns from data. With each iteration, the model fine-tunes its internal parameters to minimise the difference between its predictions and the actual outcomes. It's akin to a dancer refining each step, each posture, under the watchful eyes of an instructor until the dance mirrors the intended choreography.

Loss Functions and Gradient Descent: At the heart of this training process are two core concepts. The loss function acts as a feedback mechanism, measuring how far off a model's predictions are from the true outcomes. Gradient Descent, on the other hand, is the algorithm's guide, suggesting the direction in which adjustments should be made to minimise this loss. Picture a hiker navigating a mountainous landscape, always seeking the path downhill to find the lowest point. That's the essence of Gradient Descent.

If training is the rehearsal, inference is the performance. Once trained, the model is ready to make predictions on new, unseen data. It's the moment the curtain rises, the spotlight shines, and the dancer, having rehearsed countless times, delivers the choreography with grace and precision. Inference is about leveraging all the knowledge a model has acquired and applying it to practical scenarios.

Every artist requires tools. For the sculptor, it's the chisel and hammer; for the painter, the brush and palette. For those sculpting AI, it's data.

/imagine Behind a curtain, a dancer practices, and in front of the curtain, the same dancer performs flawlessly.

Data is the raw material from which intelligence is chiseled. It feeds into the algorithms, providing both the substance for learning and the yardstick against which predictions are measured. But not all data is equal. Quality, diversity, and volume play pivotal roles in determining its value.

Poor quality data, laden with errors and inconsistencies, can severely hamper the learning process. It's akin to a musician trying to play an out-of-tune instrument. The notes, no matter how skill-fully played, will always sound off.

Just as a writer benefits from reading a diverse range of literature, AI models thrive on diverse data. Such data ensures that the intelligence sculpted is holistic, unbiased, and well-rounded. It's the difference between seeing the world through a keyhole and viewing it atop a mountain.

In the AI realm, volume has virtue. More data often translates to more refined and accurate models. But with great volume comes great responsibility—handling, storing, and processing vast datasets demand robust infrastructure and strategic planning.

In this age, data isn't just numbers and facts—it's personal, intimate, and revealing. With data being the bedrock of AI, ethical considerations surge to the forefront. How is data collected? Is it done with consent? Is the privacy of individuals maintained? These aren't just technical queries but deeply moral ones.

As we journey deeper into the AI epoch, understanding these foundational processes—training, inference, and the nuanced relationship with data—becomes paramount. They aren't just mechanisms; they're the heartbeats that pulse through every AI system, shaping the world one prediction at a time.

Nurturing Machines - Supervised vs. Unsupervised Learning

The grandeur of Artificial Intelligence can often feel like a dazzling magic show, its wonders leaving us in awe. But like any illusion, understanding the trick unveils a world of methodology and technique. One of the central elements in this realm is the way AI learns, which can be broadly categorised into Supervised and Unsupervised Learning.

When we think of 'learning', we often think of a student and a teacher in a classroom. This paradigm forms the bedrock of the majority of AI systems today. However, this world is as diverse as the rainforests, with each technique echoing the vast biodiversity.

In the domain of Supervised Learning, AI systems play the role of students, and data acts as both the textbook and the teacher.

At the heart of supervised learning lies labeled data. These are data points accompanied by correct answers. Imagine teaching a child to recognise fruits. You show them an apple and say, "This is an apple." Here, the image is the data, and the word "apple" is the label.

Once an AI system is provided with a substantial amount of labeled data, it starts making predictions. But how do we know it's correct? By testing it against a separate set of data it hasn't seen. This process is akin to the examinations students take after a period of learning.

/imagine A sprawling rainforest, each tree representing a different learning algorithm, with some labeled trees standing tall (supervised) and some wild, unlabelled ones sprawling wide (unsupervised).

From voice recognition systems that transcribe our words to email filters that protect us from spam, supervised learning finds its application in myriad areas. These models are particularly prevalent in situations where past data can predict future events.

Challenges in Supervised Learning: However, it's not always sunny. Supervised learning faces challenges like overfitting, where a model performs exceptionally well on training data but poorly in real-world situations. There's also the challenge of acquiring high-quality labeled data, which can be time-consuming and expensive.

Unsupervised learning can be imagined as the intrepid explorer venturing into unknown terrains without a map. There are no clear answers, just patterns waiting to be discovered.

Without labels to guide them, these algorithms sift through data, seeking structures or patterns. It's akin to handing someone a jigsaw puzzle without showing them the picture it's supposed to form.

The two primary forms of unsupervised learning are clustering, where data is grouped based on similarity, and association, where patterns of co-occurrence are uncovered.

Applications in the Wild: Market segmentation, where customers are grouped based on purchasing behaviour, and recommendation systems, which suggest products or movies based on past behaviour, employ unsupervised learning.

Challenges in the Wilderness: Despite its allure, unsupervised learning is fraught with complexities. The lack of clear accuracy metrics, the potential for meaningless patterns, and the risk of over-segmentation are pitfalls that researchers grapple with.

While supervised and unsupervised learning might seem like two distinct rivers, in many scenarios, they converge, giving birth to hybrid approaches. Semi-supervised learning, for instance, uses a mix of labeled and unlabelled data.

An exciting frontier is continual learning, where AI systems learn sequentially, building on past knowledge without forgetting it—much like how we humans accumulate knowledge over our lifetimes.

As we wrap up this exploration into the paradigms of learning in AI, remember that these models are just tools. They're shaped by human hands, embodying our biases, strengths, aspirations, and flaws. As AI continues to permeate every facet of our existence, understanding these tools becomes not just an academic exercise but a societal imperative.

By diving into these waters, you've embarked on a journey of understanding, one that promises not just knowledge, but also a deeper appreciation for the dance of algorithms and data that powers our modern world.

In the cosmic dance of algorithms, understanding how they learn and evolve is akin to understanding the choreography behind a performance. The process of learning for AI closely mirrors how we humans learn, albeit at a speed and scale incomprehensible to the human brain. Our exploration delves deeper into the distinction and harmonisation of Supervised and Unsupervised Learning.

Every art form has its foundational techniques, its basics that artists return to time and again. In AI, these foundational techniques are the learning paradigms we employ. And among them, Supervised and Unsupervised Learning emerge as the twin pillars.

/imagine A machine on train tracks, smoothly running on one but derailing slightly on the other

Imagine a toddler taking their first steps, every stumble corrected by an elder's guiding hand. This is the world of supervised learning, where every attempt by the algorithm is gently directed towards correctness.

The world is awash with data, but not all data serves the purpose of supervised learning. Labeled data isn't just about names; it's about context. The richness of information accompanying each data point, the clarity of the labels, and the volume of the dataset all contribute to the learning experience.

There's a diversity in the algorithms employed in supervised learning. From linear regression, used for predicting numeric values, to decision trees that map out choices, to the complexities of neural networks that mimic human brain connections, each has its unique strength.

A significant aspect of supervised learning is optimisation. Algorithms constantly adjust their internal parameters to reduce error. This self-correction is orchestrated using various techniques like gradient descent, ensuring the algorithm hones in on the best possible solution.

The world around us brims with examples. Medical diagnostics using image recognition to identify tumours, financial systems predicting stock market fluctuations, voice assistants evolving to understand different accents — every domain feels the ripple effects of supervised learning.

Let's have a closer look at unsupervised learning. Without paths and without signboards, how would you navigate a dense forest? This is the essence of unsupervised learning. Instead of seeking predetermined answers, the algorithms hunt for hidden patterns, much like an archaeologist sifting through soil seeking relics of ancient civilisations.

Unsupervised learning thrives in ambiguity. In realms where patterns aren't immediately evident, or where the sheer volume of data is overwhelming, unsupervised techniques shine.

Often, the data we deal with has countless features. Unsupervised learning can help reduce dimensions, focusing only on the most essential features, much like condensing a long novel into a short story without losing its essence.

Unsupervised learning isn't restricted to labs and research papers. It powers content recommendations on streaming platforms, automates customer segmentation for targeted marketing, and even aids astronomers in classifying celestial bodies.

For now, we will make the Convergence: Supervised meets Unsupervised. In the complex world of AI, it's rarely a matter of choosing one over the other. More often, it's about synthesis.

Beyond the discussed paradigms lies Reinforcement Learning, a blend where agents learn by interacting with environments, drawing from both supervised and unsupervised techniques.

Many AI challenges require a multi-pronged approach. For instance, auto-encoders, a neural network architecture, use unsupervised learning to compress data and supervised learning for reconstruction.

In wrapping up this deep dive, the revelation becomes evident: AI, in all its grandeur, is still fundamentally about learning. As these systems continue to evolve, shape industries, and redefine what's possible, understanding their learning essence becomes paramount, not just for technologists, but for everyone. Because in this dance of algorithms, we're not just spectators; we're participants, choreographers, and sometimes, even the muse.

The Brain of Machines - Neural Networks and Deep Learning

The allure of replicating the human brain has long captured the imagination. Alan Turing, often remembered as the father of modern computing, pondered upon the idea of machines mimicking human intelligence. However, the real journey began in the 1940s and 50s with the introduction of the perceptron - a device intended to classify visual inputs, acting as a rudimentary neural network. But it was only in the latter half of the 20th century, with advances in computation and technology, that the deep dive into neural networks truly began.

The artificial neuron's design was heavily inspired by its biological counterpart. In our brains, each neuron connects to others through structures called synapses. These synapses carry signals, which are then processed by the neuron. Similarly, in an artificial setup, each neuron receives a certain value, multiplies it with a 'weight', adds a 'bias', and then processes this through an activation function.

Imagine for a moment, a vast metropolis at night. Each light in the skyline is akin to a neuron. Some lights (or neurones) are brighter, signalling more activity. Others are dimmer, indicating less action. This radiant dance of luminosity is reminiscent of how neurones in a neural network function, each determining its output based on its input and internal logic.

Imagine a cascading waterfall, with each drop of water representing a piece of data. As this data descends, it gets transformed. At the top, it's raw and unprocessed. But as it moves down layer by layer, it gets refined, transformed, and purified.

This is how layered neural networks operate. The early layers might recognise simple patterns, like lines or colours. As data moves deeper, these patterns assemble into more complex structures. By the final layers, the network is capable of recognising intricate patterns, such as faces in images or emotions in text.

As computers became more powerful, the depth and breadth of these networks expanded, birthing Deep Learning. If the early neural networks were like small ponds, deep learning models are vast, intricate oceans.

To illustrate generative adversarial networks (GANs), imagine two artists in a contest. One creates a painting, while the other critiques it. The first artist then refines their work based on the feedback, and this loop continues until a masterpiece is formed. In the world of AI, GANs operate similarly. One network generates data, and another evaluates it. Together, they refine the output, enabling the creation of near-realistic images, music, and even text.

Transfer learning we shall understand as instead of training a deep learning model from scratch, what if we could transfer the knowledge of one model to another? This concept, akin to a seasoned chef imparting his skills to an apprentice, has significantly reduced training times and computational resources, allowing for rapid advancements in various AI applications.

While neural networks and deep learning promise a

/imagine A visual of a circuit board, with highlighted areas showcasing GPU and TPU chips.

transformative impact, they are not without challenges. Overfitting, where a model becomes too tailored to the training data, forgetting the generalised knowledge, is a recurring issue. Solutions like dropout, where random

107

neurones are turned off during training, serve as countermeasures.

Moreover, the vast computational resources required for these networks have spurred innovations in hardware. The rise of Graphics Processing Units (GPUs) and Tensor Processing Units (TPUs) tailored for neural computations is a testament to the intertwined evolution of hardware and AI.

The capabilities of deep learning models, especially in areas like facial recognition, have brought forth ethical considerations. How do we ensure the unbiased operation of these models? How do we value privacy while leveraging the power of AI? These questions are becoming central in today's AI discussions.

To fully appreciate neural networks and deep learning, one must not only delve into their technical depths but also understand their societal implications. As these AI models become increasingly prevalent in our world, striking the right balance between their potential and the inherent responsibilities becomes crucial.

PART 3

Rethinking Computing Architectures for AI

AlexNet and its Significance in Machine Learning Progression

Developed by three researchers from the University of Toronto, AlexNet is marked a critical turning point in machine learning. This deep learning algorithm showcased its capabilities during the ImageNet competition, which tests algorithms on image recognition tasks using a vast dataset sourced and labeled by Mechanical Turk contributors.

Before AlexNet's introduction, most algorithms struggled to achieve high accuracy in image recognition. However, AlexNet substantially improved the performance, reducing error rates from 25% to 15%. This achievement represented significant progress in the domain of artificial intelligence.

The researchers leveraged convolutional neural networks, a type of neural network previously overlooked due to perceived computational limitations. They used CUDA for programming, benefiting from the parallel processing capabilities of GPUs. By doing so, they could efficiently train their neural networks on cost-effective, consumer-grade hardware. The key to this achievement was exploiting the

GPU's capacity for executing multiple instructions simultaneously, which optimised the algorithm's processing capabilities.

Nvidia's graphic cards were instrumental in this advancement. Beyond graphics rendering, they enabled parallel computation, essential for AI, cryptocurrency, and other applications that heavily depend on linear algebra and matrix math operations. By offloading these computations from CPUs to GPUs, processes were markedly accelerated.

Companies like Google and Facebook rapidly adopted and adapted the principles behind AlexNet. This led to advancements in targeted advertising algorithms and significantly increased the value of platforms such as Instagram. For instance, Google refined its YouTube algorithms, which significantly influenced user engagement metrics like autoplay and feed recommendations.

While AlexNet was foundational, the technology landscape began consolidating around a few major entities, primarily Google and Facebook, drawing in top AI researchers. Although substantial progress was achieved, the industry remained far from realising genuine human-equivalent artificial intelligence. AlexNet served as a precursor to more advanced AI models and techniques that would emerge.

In conclusion, while AlexNet represented a major stride in AI, the field is continually evolving. The overarching narrative is one of rapid advancement and consolidation, with future developments poised to further shape the AI landscape.

In Silicon Valley, there was a growing sentiment that Google and Facebook's dominance in AI could present considerable obstacles. This perspective was not yet widespread among the general populace. This insight was not just an issue for their tech giant peers; it indicated potential global implications. In comparison, companies like Apple trailed significantly in their AI capabilities, making them less competitive in the consumer market.

There were multiple layers of concern:

Major tech companies found it challenging to compete.

Startups faced an uphill battle, contending with giants like Google and Facebook during an era where AI propelled tech innovation. These startups, such as Snap, had difficulties matching the likes of Facebook. Others, like Musical.ly, were acquired by bigger corporations like ByteDance, potentially due to gaps in business strategy, implementation, or access to cutting-edge AI research, leading to the emergence of TikTok.

A broader societal issue was the potential stagnation in AI progress due to talent concentration within Google and Facebook. This prompted the creation of OpenAI, aiming to reach Artificial General Intelligence (AGI) ahead of these tech giants. The philosophy behind OpenAI was that the first entity to achieve AGI would have immense power, which should be vested in impartial hands.

In 2015, a crucial meeting took place at the Rosewood Hotel on Sand Hill Road. Elon Musk and Sam Altman convened this gathering to entice top AI researchers from Google and Facebook to contribute to their mission of breaking this duopoly. Most offers were declined, with many researchers preferring their current affiliations, competitive pay packages, and collaborations with leading AI experts, which they believed they might miss in disjointed academic contexts.

Yet, Ilya Sutskever displayed interest in Elon and Sam's proposal, eventually departing Google to help establish

OpenAI, a standalone nonprofit AI research organisation, despite apparent risks. This venture marked a unique path, differing from the initial growth narratives of firms such as Nvidia.

While OpenAI's genesis was not straightforward, it has since evolved over eight years, producing innovations like ChatGPT. A critical partner in this journey, Crusoe, a green compute cloud provider, focuses on AI workloads. They harness technologies like the 3200 gigabit InfiniBand and

/imagine An intricately designed clockwork mechanism with cogs and wheels, each representing a different algorithm, working in unison

collaborate with Nvidia to maximise AI training cluster performance. They prioritise eco-friendliness, using stranded or green energy, delivering cost-effective solutions.

This account underscores the early challenges and eventual formation of OpenAI, emphasising the range of hurdles and innovations in AI. It highlights the importance of challenging monopolies for tech progression and societal betterment.

The subsequent version boasted an impressive 175 billion parameters. Moreover, newer, more sophisticated models pushed boundaries, processing even larger volumes of data. The expenses involved in training these models skyrocketed, demanding extensive computational power, dedicated hardware, and significant energy consumption.

Examining the development of these models, GPT-3 presented an expanded set of capabilities, enhancing adaptability and responsiveness to varied inputs. It could discern the intricacies of natural language impressively, becoming an invaluable asset in numerous applications like chatbots, translation, and content generation.

However, the enhancements weren't solely due to model size. Improvements in algorithms and structural design were crucial in boosting the models' efficiency and performance. Breakthroughs in attention mechanisms, parameter sharing, and optimisation algorithms bolstered the models' learning capabilities, enabling them to adeptly manage a multitude of language-related tasks.

As the technology advanced at a blistering pace, researchers continuously expanded the frontiers of language model capabilities, aiming for deeper contextual understanding, managing longer text sequences, and yielding more contextually appropriate responses.

However, this progression was rife with complexities. As models expanded, the supporting infrastructure had to be more advanced and elaborate. Tireless efforts went into designing scalable solutions that met the needs of advanced models, augmenting their capabilities while controlling increasing costs.

It was evident that sheer size wouldn't resolve all natural language processing obstacles. There was a concerted push to design models keenly aware of language's subtle nuances, its sociocultural contexts, and the myriad ways meanings manifest and are perceived.

Rather than solely relying on generic internet content, these models incorporated diverse linguistic forms, ranging from literature to academic writings, equipping them to discern and reproduce a broader range of human expression and wisdom.

Moreover, as AI advanced, ethical deliberations took center stage. With the growing influence of larger models, addressing inherent biases became paramount. Intense discussions and significant effort went into developing fairer, more impartial, and conscientious models.

Additionally, OpenAI and similar bodies began partnering more openly with external stakeholders, merging insights from fields like linguistics, cognitive science, and ethics to craft models more attuned to human values and societal requisites.

Entities like OpenAI were not merely focused on creating advanced models. They also ventured into the relatively unexplored domain of ethical AI development, addressing issues of responsibility, transparency, and AI's long-term societal repercussions.

The AI sector was increasingly acknowledging these technologies' transformative effects, striving to ensure AI's development and utilisation remained advantageous and equitable for all.

To sum up, AI's trajectory, from its inception to today's advanced language models, is characterised by incessant innovation, discovery, and introspection. It's not just about pioneering models with unmatched capabilities, but also comprehending the deep implications and obligations accompanying such influence.

This journey is ongoing, with every innovation ushering in novel opportunities and challenges, and each introspection fostering a more profound comprehension of our inventions and our very essence. AI's odyssey is still unfolding, and the pursuit for smarter, more compassionate, and accountable models persists, shaping both technology's and humanity's futures.

As time went on, the alliance between OpenAI and Microsoft deepened, evolving into a stronger and more multifaceted partnership. The meteoric rise of transformer models wove a complex narrative of innovations, becoming indispensable in a variety of applications, some outside their initial envisioned scope.

Following the launch of GPT-4, a transformative shift was palpable in the tech arena. The sheer scale of this model, combined with the vast resources from collaborative ventures, unveiled a spectrum of new potentialities. GPT-4 transitioned from a mere text generator to a force propelling breakthroughs in fields like healthcare, education, and ecological research. Developers harnessed its power in applications that addressed real-world challenges and amplified human potential.

Yet, with the widespread adoption of such advanced models, critical concerns about ethics, privacy, and the digital disparity emerged. As tech powerhouses like Google and Microsoft delved deeper into AI, the importance of ethically crafting and utilising these technologies was spotlighted. Numerous advocacy groups and ethicists championed for clearness, equity, and responsibility in AI undertakings to guarantee a fair allocation of benefits while averting negative ramifications.

The depth and intricacy of AI models spurred an avid quest for cutting-edge, efficient hardware. Firms evolved from being mere consumers of hardware from providers like Nvidia, instead forging alliances or even crafting custom hardware to accommodate their burgeoning AI requirements. This catalysed a fresh surge of hardware technological leaps, redefining the limits of processing capacity and efficacy.

Simultaneously, while cherishing its rewarding partnership with Microsoft, OpenAI expanded its horizon, forming ties with various organisations, scholars, and academic bodies. This AI titan funded and engaged in research endeavours to chart new terrains of AI, aspiring to discover innovative approaches that could bolster AI model proficiencies.

GPT-4's unparalleled prowess accentuated cloud computing's pivotal role. The availability and adaptability offered by cloud platforms became vital for nascent companies and startups eager to exploit top-tier AI models. This democratised high-caliber computational access, inviting a broad spectrum of pioneers to enrich the dynamic AI domain. The fusion of cloud technology with AI began reshaping commercial paradigms, spawning a myriad of novel services and platforms.

Further, collaborations between Microsoft and OpenAI evolved with more encompassing aspirations, focusing on crafting AI capable of assimilating multimodal data, merging visual, auditory, and textual information to birth advanced, holistic models. They aspired to design AI that went beyond text comprehension, aiming for a human-like perceptual ability.

The interplay between OpenAI and Microsoft only intensified over time, moulding a potent coalition steering AI's course. However, they both prized inclusivity, inviting the global tech community to join, innovate, and enrich, cultivating a vibrant, varied, and inclusive technological milieu.

In this ongoing AI narrative, the horizons appeared limitless. The confluence of powerful entities, intellectual brilliance, and state-of-the-art tech envisaged a future where AI transcended being a mere instrument, becoming a partner in humanity's endless odyssey of exploration and invention. The entwined journeys of OpenAI, Microsoft, and their contemporaries transcended mere rivalry and technological dominance; they painted a vision of a future where tech and humans harmoniously thrive and prosper.

Recognising the Potential of Generative AI

The initial recognition that generative AI is not only a possibility but is also gaining traction was pivotal. When you think about the enormous GPU computation required for this training, the natural evolution for such a computational demand is the cloud. This shift towards the cloud represents a significant moment in the timeline of technological advancement.

In the early 2000s, the idea of generative AI was mostly speculative, confined to the pages of academic journals and the imaginations of forward-thinking engineers. Many dismissed these initial musings as overly optimistic or even far-fetched. The computational power required for these models seemed unreachable with the hardware of that era.

Nvidia, a company that was primarily known for its graphics processing units (GPUs) for gaming, saw the bigger picture. While their GPUs were recognised for rendering detailed and dynamic graphics, the underlying architecture had the potential for so much more. The parallel processing capability, the bedrock of their GPUs, was a match made in heaven for the demands of AI computations.

Jensen Huang, the CEO and co-founder of Nvidia, often spoke about this transformative potential in the company's early days. While many saw GPUs as tools for rendering lifelike gaming experiences, Huang saw them as the foundation for the next computing revolution. He recognised the latent potential of GPUs for much broader applications, way beyond gaming.

However, the journey from this vision to realisation was not without its bumps. Initial forays into AI-related hardware by other companies often prioritised task-specific architectures. This means that the hardware was narrowly designed to perform specific tasks, but these architectures lacked the versatility that AI's evolving landscape demanded. Nvidia's GPU architecture, on the other hand, was inherently versatile, which positioned it as a more sustainable solution for the unpredictable evolution of AI.

Early on, Nvidia began investing in research to tweak its GPUs for AI workloads. They worked closely with researchers and academic institutions to understand the computational challenges that emerging AI algorithms posed. These collaborative efforts bore fruit in the form of CUDA, a parallel computing platform and API model created by Nvidia. CUDA allowed developers to use Nvidia GPUs for general purpose processing (an approach known as GPGPU, General-Purpose computing on Graphics Processing Units).

This was a pivotal moment in the AI landscape. With CUDA, AI researchers could now harness the power of GPUs to train increasingly complex models. The development of neural networks and deep learning models, which demanded parallel processing capabilities, suddenly became more feasible and faster. Nvidia's foresight in developing CUDA effectively democratised AI research, enabling many researchers to experiment and iterate their models without requiring supercomputing facilities.

Around the same time, the broader tech industry began to take note of the advancements in cloud computing. The cloud offered a scalable solution to businesses, providing computational resources on demand. For Nvidia, the cloud presented another significant opportunity. If AI was the software of the future, then cloud-based GPU infrastructure would be the hardware driving it.

The company began strategic partnerships with leading cloud providers to ensure that Nvidia GPUs became the backbone of AI cloud infrastructure. This was not merely a business move; it was a strategic play to position Nvidia at the very heart of the AI revolution.

Indeed, as generative models started gaining prominence, the need for more extensive training data and more powerful computational resources became evident. These models required not only more extensive datasets but also vast amounts of computation to churn through this data and generate meaningful patterns. Traditional CPU-based data centres couldn't keep up. Here, again, Nvidia's GPUs, with their parallel processing capabilities, proved invaluable.

AI start-ups began cropping up globally, and the importance of having accessible and scalable GPU resources became paramount. With Nvidia GPUs available on the cloud, these start-ups could access top-tier computational resources without hefty initial investments, levelling the playing field and fostering innovation.

Beyond the start-up world, established tech giants also started taking notice. Companies like Google, Microsoft, and Amazon began integrating Nvidia GPUs into their cloud solutions. These partnerships not only validated Nvidia's strategy but also solidified its position as a dominant force in the AI hardware landscape.

The brilliance of Nvidia's approach was multi-faceted. They didn't just develop a product and wait for the market to catch up. Instead, they actively fostered an ecosystem around their products. Through academic partnerships, developer workshops, and open-source contributions, Nvidia ensured that the next generation of AI researchers and developers were familiar with their tools and platforms.

The company also invested in AI research directly, funding projects, and collaborating with researchers to push the boundaries of what was possible. This was not just about market dominance; it was about shaping the future of the field.

As the years rolled on, the importance of Nvidia's contributions to the AI community became undeniably clear. The landscape of artificial intelligence, particularly generative AI, might have looked vastly different without Nvidia's hardware innovations and collaborative spirit.

In conclusion, while generative AI's concept seemed distant and unattainable in the early 2000s, Nvidia's strategic moves, combined with its belief in the transformative power of GPUs, brought it to the forefront. The company's journey serves as a testament to the importance of vision, collaboration, and adaptability in the ever-evolving tech world.

As Nvidia firmly positioned itself at the forefront of the AI computational revolution, a new set of challenges and opportunities began to emerge. AI, especially in the form of deep learning, was no longer just a niche topic of research. It was finding applications in numerous industries, from healthcare and finance to entertainment and automotive.

With the onset of AI's commercialisation, Nvidia faced the challenge of diversifying its offerings. The company couldn't rest on the laurels of its GPUs; it had to innovate further, not just to maintain its leadership but also to cater to the nuanced demands of different industries.

The automotive industry was one of the first to recognise the transformative potential of AI. Self-driving cars, once a concept of science fiction, were becoming a tangible reality. Companies like Tesla were at the forefront of this revolution, but they needed powerful computational hardware to process the vast amounts of data their sensors collected in real-time. Recognising this need, Nvidia launched the Drive platform—a combination of hardware and software tailor-made for autonomous vehicles.

But it wasn't just about raw computational power. Safety, reliability, and efficiency were crucial in the automotive sector. Nvidia had to ensure that its platforms could process data swiftly, make decisions in split seconds, and do so consistently without failures. The company heavily invested in research and formed partnerships with car manufacturers, ensuring that its Drive platform would be robust enough for the challenges of the open road.

The healthcare sector was another area where AI was making significant strides. From medical imaging to drug discovery, the potential applications of AI in healthcare were vast. However, these applications also came with their unique set of challenges. For one, the stakes in healthcare were high. Errors could lead to misdiagnoses, delayed treatments, or even loss of life. Furthermore, healthcare data was sensitive, and its handling required strict privacy and security measures.

Nvidia, understanding these intricacies, introduced Clara —a platform designed specifically for healthcare applications. Clara was not just about processing power; it was about ensuring that AI models in healthcare were accurate, interpretable, and secure.

However, as Nvidia expanded its horizons, it also had to grapple with increasing competition. Companies like AMD, Intel, and even Google with its Tensor Processing Units (TPUs) were eager to carve out a slice of the booming AI hardware market. Nvidia's early entry gave it a head start, but maintaining its leadership required continuous innovation and adaptability.

One of the significant challenges Nvidia faced was the ever-evolving landscape of AI algorithms. The models were becoming deeper and more complex, requiring even more computational power. To address this, Nvidia began developing specialised hardware like the Tensor Cores, specifically designed to accelerate deep learning training and inference.

Environmental concerns also began to shape the tech industry's landscape. With massive data centres worldwide running round the clock, the carbon footprint of the AI revolution was significant. Nvidia recognised its responsibility in this regard and started initiatives to make its GPUs more energy-efficient and promote sustainable practices in AI research and applications.

Another avenue that Nvidia explored was edge computing. With devices like smartphones, drones, and IoT devices becoming increasingly intelligent, there was a need to process data locally rather than in distant data centers. Nvidia's Jetson platform catered to this very need, offering powerful AI computation capabilities in compact, energy-efficient packages suitable for edge devices.

A panorama of scenes ranging from someone binge-watching a series, a marketer analysing customer clusters, to telescopes aimed at the night sky.

The rise of quantum computing, often hailed as the next frontier in computational technology, presented both a challenge and an opportunity. While quantum computers have the potential to revolutionise various industries, they also threatened to make classical computers, including GPUs, obsolete for specific tasks. Nvidia, always with an eye on the future, began investing in research to understand how GPUs could coexist with, and even complement, quantum machines.

In reflection, the journey of Nvidia in the AI era, particularly during its expansion phase, highlights the intricate dance between innovation, adaptation, and foresight. The company's ability to anticipate industry needs, diversify its offerings, and remain committed to research and collaboration has solidified its place in the annals of tech history. As AI continues to shape the future, Nvidia's role in its evolution will undoubtedly be remembered as pivotal.

The Global Impact and the Ethical Frontiers

With the advancement of AI and the pivotal role Nvidia played in its maturation, global implications emerged that transcended technical challenges. The world was no longer simply concerned with how fast a model could be trained, but also with the broader societal and ethical impact of these technologies.

The ubiquity of AI in various sectors inadvertently led to a discourse about its implications on employment. There were fears that as automation became more prevalent, many traditional jobs would become obsolete. While Nvidia was at the heart of enabling AI's capabilities, it recognised the need to be part of the solution. In response, the company initiated and supported various educational programs aimed at reskilling workers, ensuring they remained relevant in an AI-driven landscape.

However, the challenges were not solely economic. There were significant ethical quandaries. The AI models, especially those in the realm of deep learning, were essentially black boxes. Even with the incredible computational prowess of Nvidia's GPUs, there was no guarantee that the AI's decision-making process was transparent or understandable to humans. This lack of interpretability posed risks, especially in sectors like healthcare or criminal justice, where understanding the rationale behind decisions could be a matter of life and death.

To address this, Nvidia collaborated with research institutions globally to promote the development of explainable AI (XAI) frameworks. They endeavoured to make AI models more transparent, ensuring that their decision-making processes could be understood and interrogated.

Furthermore, concerns about bias in AI models became a hotbed of debate. If the data fed to train these models was biased, the models would perpetuate those biases, potentially leading to unfair or discriminatory outcomes. Nvidia, realising its influential position, championed the cause of fair and unbiased AI. The company began organising symposiums and workshops, bringing together researchers, ethicists, and industry professionals to collaboratively address the challenge of bias in AI.

Environmental implications, which started becoming more pronounced during Nvidia's expansion phase, took center stage. Recognising the vast energy consumption of data centres worldwide, Nvidia took strides toward sustainability. They unveiled initiatives aiming for carbon-neutral operations and developed hardware optimised for energy efficiency, without compromising performance.

The global nature of Nvidia's operations meant the company also had to navigate geopolitical complexities. With countries striving to achieve AI supremacy, the sale and export of Nvidia's high-powered GPUs became tightly regulated. The company had to strategically balance its global expansion aspirations with compliance to international regulations and norms.

Amidst all these challenges, Nvidia's commitment to open-source contributions was unwavering. Recognising that the collective intelligence of the global developer community was pivotal for the responsible advancement of AI, Nvidia continued to release tools, libraries, and frameworks to the public domain, fostering collaboration and shared growth.

Another significant area that Nvidia ventured into was the realm of AI ethics. Collaborating with philosophers, sociologists, and ethicists, Nvidia was at the forefront of drafting ethical guidelines for AI research and deployment. They stressed the importance of developing AI systems that aligned with human values, ensuring that as these systems became more autonomous, they remained beneficial to humanity.

In conclusion, Nvidia's journey in the AI era underscores the multi-faceted challenges faced by tech giants in the modern world. Beyond mere technological hurdles, Nvidia had to grapple with societal, ethical, and geopolitical complexities. By proactively addressing these challenges and fostering global collaboration, Nvidia showcased that technological advancement and ethical responsibility were not mutually exclusive but could coexist harmoniously. As the AI saga continues to unfold, Nvidia's legacy will be a testament to this delicate yet crucial balance.

The AI epoch, championed by Nvidia's contributions, had reshaped the technology industry and had profound implications across myriad sectors. However, with each milestone Nvidia achieved, new challenges loomed on the horizon. The company, while basking in its success, was acutely aware that resting on its laurels would be detrimental in the rapidly evolving landscape.

One of the first challenges that Nvidia faced was the

/imagine A massive library with endless shelves of unsorted, unlabelled books, representing the vastness of unlabelled data.

emergence of quantum computing. Experts touted quantum computers as the next big leap, potentially dwarfing classical computing's capabilities, including the advanced AI models that Nvidia's GPUs supported. The quantum realm's promise to solve problems deemed unsolvable by classical computers posed a direct challenge to Nvidia's dominance.

To navigate this, Nvidia began investing in hybrid models, where classical GPUs would work in tandem with quantum processors. These efforts aimed to bridge the gap between the two worlds, leveraging the strengths of both quantum and classical methods. Early collaborations with quantum research facilities hinted at the enormous potential of such synergistic endeavours.

Another challenge arose from the growth of edge computing. As devices became smarter, there was an increasing need to process data locally rather than in distant data centres. This decentralised approach posed questions about Nvidia's server-based GPU model. Recognising this shift, Nvidia started focusing on producing efficient, smaller-scale GPUs tailored for edge devices, ensuring that AI processing could happen seamlessly, whether on a remote server or a local device.

The rise of customised AI chips, developed by tech behemoths like Google's Tensor Processing Units (TPUs) and Apple's Neural Engine, also signalled competition. These companies started building hardware optimised for their specific software needs. Nvidia, in response, began broadening its ecosystem. They not only developed GPUs but also ventured into creating a holistic AI platform, ensuring that they remained a one-stop solution for all AI needs, regardless of the application.

Ethically, as AI models became more complex and powerful, there were growing concerns about super-intelligent AI. The fear that an uncontrolled AI system might surpass human intelligence and act in unpredictable ways became a hot topic of debate. Nvidia, realising its responsibility, began funding research into AI safety, ensuring that precautionary measures were in place to prevent any potential runaway scenarios.

Lastly, the company faced challenges from emerging markets. Countries like China and India, with their vast pools of engineering talent and growing tech industries, started fostering homegrown companies specialising in AI hardware. Nvidia had to innovate not just technologically but also in its business strategies to remain relevant and competitive in these rapidly growing markets.

In wrapping up, it's clear that Nvidia's journey was not a straight path to success. The landscape was riddled with technological evolutions, competitive challenges, and ethical dilemmas. But if history were any indicator, Nvidia's adaptability and commitment to innovation positioned it well to face the future, no matter how uncertain.

With every challenge that the future held, Nvidia's story served as a beacon for tech enthusiasts, ethicists, and businesses worldwide. It exemplified the essence of innovation, the responsibility of leadership, and the relentless pursuit of a vision, even in the face of adversity.

Nvidia's rise and its subsequent achievements in the AI era didn't merely represent the success of a single corporation. Instead, it became emblematic of the broader evolution of the tech industry and the global implications of this shift. We delve into the societal, educational, and industry-wide impacts spurred by Nvidia's dominance.

On a societal level, Nvidia's contributions to AI led to the creation of technologies that once seemed the stuff of science fiction. Advanced healthcare diagnostics, real-time language translation, smart cities optimised for sustainability, and personalised educational platforms — all became tangible realities. The GPU technology, once a mere tool for rendering lifelike graphics in video games, now lay at the heart of tools improving the quality of life for millions around the world.

In the realm of education, Nvidia's innovations led to a renewed focus on computational studies. Universities and colleges across the globe began offering specialised courses in GPU programming, deep learning, and AI-specific hardware design. Nvidia itself initiated several educational programs, scholarships, and partnerships with academic institutions, aiming to nurture the next generation of tech innovators. These efforts ensured a continuous supply of skilled professionals well-versed in the latest technologies.

For the broader tech industry, Nvidia's story served as both an inspiration and a cautionary tale. Startups and established companies alike began to realise the value of foresight and adaptability. While technological prowess was essential, so was the ability to anticipate industry shifts and respond accordingly. Many businesses started investing heavily in R&D, not just to keep up with the present but to prepare for the challenges of the future.

However, Nvidia's dominance also brought forth questions about monopolies and the concentration of power. With so much influence in the AI hardware sector, concerns arose about stifling competition and potential barriers to entry for newcomers. Regulatory bodies and watchdogs became increasingly vigilant, ensuring that the playing field remained level and that innovation wasn't stifled.

On the environmental front, Nvidia's high-performance GPUs, essential for AI research, consumed significant amounts of energy. This drew attention to the environmental footprint of large-scale AI operations. In response, Nvidia began initiatives focused on creating energy-efficient chips and promoting sustainable AI research practices, reinforcing the idea that technological advancement and environmental responsibility could go hand-in-hand.

Finally, the company's legacy was felt in the realm of collaboration. Nvidia's success wasn't just its own; it was intricately linked with tech developers, researchers, and businesses that utilised their GPUs. This interdependence fostered an environment of collaboration, with Nvidia often working closely with other entities to optimise AI solutions. Such collaborations exemplified the future of tech — one not dominated by solitary giants but characterised by a network of symbiotic relationships.

Nvidia's impact extended far beyond its financial success or technological innovations. It reshaped industries, influenced educational trajectories, and set new standards for corporate responsibility. The story of Nvidia in the AI era was not just about one company's journey but about the tapestry of change that it wove across the global landscape.

PART 4

The Grand Convergence

Global Cloud - Ultimate Repository of Human Knowledge

Digital renaissance of the 21st century was characterised by breathtaking innovations, and at the forefront was the idea that would change the landscape of technology: cloud computing. It was in these early years of the millennium that the concept of the cloud began to take shape, transcending its initial intangible nature to become a defining part of our digital lives.

Historically, data and software were rigidly tethered to the physical devices they were installed on. As our reliance on digital data grew exponentially, so did the limitations of this model. Computers crashed, hard drives corrupted, and valuable data was lost to the ether. The solution, many believed, lay in the idea of 'off-site' storage.

The initial cloud was simple, yet revolutionary. Instead of storing data on an individual's personal computer, it could be uploaded to a server and accessed via the internet. This seemingly mundane shift laid the foundation for what would evolve into today's intricate web of cloud services. As internet speeds accelerated and connectivity issues diminished, cloud technologies expanded from mere storage solutions to platforms that could run entire software applications, host databases, and power massive online operations. What began as a convenient backup method metamorphosed into the backbone of global enterprises.

Companies like Salesforce pioneered Software as a Service (SaaS), allowing businesses to operate without the need for on-site software installations. Then came the development of Infrastructure as a Service (IaaS) and Platform as a Service (PaaS), heralding a new era where not just software, but even the underlying infrastructure and platforms could be rented out. With this evolution, businesses could scale up or down based on demand, without the substantial upfront costs of physical infrastructure.

Like all new frontiers, the early days of cloud computing were fraught with challenges. The freedom and flexibility promised by the cloud came with its set of obstacles. High latency, concerns about data loss, and questions about reliability were but a few of the teething problems. For many businesses, especially those operating in regions with less developed internet infrastructures, trusting the cloud seemed a risk too great.

However, these challenges also presented an opportunity —an opportunity seized by the tech behemoths. Companies like Amazon, Microsoft, and Google identified the immense potential in this fledgling technology. By leveraging their vast resources, they embarked on ambitious projects to reshape the cloud landscape.

Amazon Web Services (AWS) spearheaded the movement, offering a suite of tools that catered to both budding startups and established corporations. Microsoft, not to be outdone, unveiled Azure, integrating seamlessly with its vast array of software products. Google Cloud, with its emphasis on open platforms and cutting-edge innovations, brought a fresh perspective to the table.

These big players not only revolutionised the way cloud services were delivered but also played a pivotal role in building trust. Through robust security measures, constant upgrades, and a commitment to reliability, they showcased the cloud's potential and paved the way for its widespread adoption. As these giants battled for supremacy, innovation flourished, resulting in a richer, more mature cloud ecosystem that reshaped industries and defined the modern digital age.

As the convenience and efficiency of the cloud became increasingly embedded in daily life, from personal photo storage to enterprise-scale operations, public perceptions underwent a profound transformation. Initially, the very concept of the cloud was nebulous to many. People grappled with the idea of entrusting their data, a representation of their personal or professional lives, to an unseen entity. There were myriad concerns – what if their data got lost? Or worse, what if it was accessed by unintended individuals or entities?

Over time, as interactions with the cloud became routine, concerns pivoted from the mere act of storing data offsite to the implications of such actions. High-profile data breaches and stories of companies misusing personal information for targeted advertising made headlines. The narrative shifted from 'Can we trust the cloud?' to 'How is our data being used, and who has access to it?' This public scrutiny placed pressure on companies to prioritise data privacy, leading to a renewed focus on encryption, multi-factor authentication, and comprehensive data policies.

Data privacy concerns also catalysed significant legislative action. Regulations like the General Data Protection Regulation (GDPR) in Europe and the California Consumer Privacy Act (CCPA) in the U.S. set new standards for data protection, granting consumers greater control over their personal information. These laws not only provided a framework for businesses but also helped in refining public perception, making consumers more aware and informed about their digital rights.

Amid the debates surrounding data privacy, it's essential not to lose sight of the transformative benefits the cloud has ushered in. One of the most profound of these benefits is the concept of unified knowledge. By storing and making accessible vast amounts of data in real-time, the cloud has revolutionised our approach to knowledge sharing and collaboration.

In academia and research, cloud platforms have enabled scholars from diverse geographical locations to collaborate in real-time, sharing data sets, research findings, and methodologies instantly. This collaborative approach has accelerated the pace of research in fields ranging from astrophysics to molecular biology.

Beyond the world of academia, shared global knowledge has transformed everyday life. For instance, medical professionals across the world can now access case studies, latest research, and even complex medical imagery, all in real-time. This has not only refined diagnostic and treatment methodologies but has also democratised access to cutting-edge medical knowledge.

The implications of this unified approach to knowledge extend to areas like environmental science, where global collaborative initiatives leverage the cloud to track climate patterns, deforestation rates, and ocean temperatures. By having a centralised repository of data that can be accessed and updated in real-time, scientists, policymakers, and activists can craft more informed strategies to combat global challenges.

Similarly, in the realm of education, the cloud has been a game-changer. Online educational platforms, MOOCs (Massive Open Online Courses), and digital libraries have broken geographical barriers, making quality education accessible to anyone with an internet connection. The dream of a globally educated population, with access to the same quality of resources, is slowly inching closer to reality, all thanks to the global cloud.

The ascent of the global cloud was not without its perils. As the vast expanse of interconnected servers held increasing amounts of sensitive information, it became a tantalising target for hackers, cybercriminals, and even nation-states. The potential rewards for infiltrating these systems were immense, and as a result, the frequency and sophistication of cyberattacks surged.

High-profile data breaches exposed the personal information of millions, sometimes even billions, of individuals. Financial data, health records, and even intimate personal details became a commodity on the dark web. The aftermath of such breaches often resulted in financial losses, damaged reputations for corporations, and a sense of vulnerability among the public.

Beyond individual hackers and organised cybercrime groups, the cloud became a battleground for state-sponsored cyber warfare. Nation-states recognised the strategic advantage of infiltrating not just the digital infrastructure of their adversaries but also the vast repositories of data. Espionage, sabotage, and even influence operations were conducted under the veil of the digital realm, leveraging the interconnected nature of the cloud.

While these challenges cast a shadow over the promise of the cloud, they also catalysed innovations in cybersecurity. The digital arms race had begun, and at its core was the cloud, the most significant repository of human knowledge.

/imagine A painting of two towering pillars, each adorned with symbols of data and algorithms, standing firm amidst a swirling cosmos of information.

Amid the cybersecurity threats, another critical concern emerged – the concentration of power in the hands of a few tech giants. As cloud services grew in scale and reach, a few key players began to dominate the landscape. Companies like Amazon, Google, Microsoft, and a handful of others held a disproportionate amount of the world's digital data.

This monopolistic control over data raised several ethical concerns. For one, these corporations had unparalleled insight into the behaviours, preferences, and interactions of billions of people. This data wasn't just used to refine services and offer better products; it was also leveraged to influence behaviours, shape perceptions, and in some cases, even sway public opinion.

Furthermore, these data monopolies often acted as gatekeepers. While they did offer tools and platforms for innovation, there were also instances where they stifled competition, either by acquiring emerging competitors or by leveraging their vast resources to overshadow them.

The role of these tech giants in the global cloud ecosystem raised pertinent questions about equity, control, and the very nature of the internet. Was the dream of a decentralised web, where knowledge was democratised and power was distributed, being overshadowed by these emerging digital empires? The debate was just beginning, and the implications were profound, shaping the trajectory of the cloud and its role in society.

As the power and influence of cloud technology magnified, governments around the world began to recognise the necessity of intervening. Initially, many states were passive observers, somewhat ill-equipped to understand the rapid technological changes. But as the implications of data monopolies and breaches became clear, there was a significant push to develop comprehensive frameworks to regulate the digital sphere.

In Europe, the General Data Protection Regulation (GDPR) was one of the first and most comprehensive efforts to give citizens control over their data. This legislation mandated clear consent for data collection and granted individuals the right to access, rectify, or delete their data. Companies faced stringent fines if they violated these regulations, marking a significant shift in the balance of power from corporations back to individuals.

In other parts of the world, nations grappled with the dual challenge of fostering innovation while ensuring data protection. Countries like India and Brazil introduced their data protection laws, balancing the rights of citizens with the needs of a growing digital economy.

However, not all government interventions were welcomed. In some regions, state control over the cloud was seen as a means to stifle dissent, control information flow, and suppress freedom of expression. The fine line between regulation and repression became a global debate, with the cloud at its epicentre.

With the immense value and sensitivity of data stored in the global cloud, ensuring its security became paramount. While tech giants invested heavily in cybersecurity measures, national governments also played a crucial role in safeguarding their digital territories.

National data sovereignty laws began to emerge, demanding that data generated within a country's borders be stored domestically. For countries like China and Russia, these laws were not only about security but also about control over information and maintaining an upper hand in the global digital race.

Simultaneously, the evolution of cybersecurity became intertwined with advancements in artificial intelligence. AI-driven threat detection systems, real-time breach alerts, and automated security patches became standard tools in the fight against cyber threats. But this integration also raised concerns. As AI systems became gatekeepers of the global cloud, questions about their transparency, accountability, and potential biases took center stage.

In this era, the global cloud was not just a technological marvel; it was a geopolitical entity, a domain where nations asserted their dominance, negotiated their boundaries, and collaborated for a shared digital future. The quest for security and sovereignty in the digital realm would shape the next phase of the global cloud's evolution.

The centralisation of data in the hands of a few tech giants had long been a point of contention. As the importance of the cloud grew, so did the concerns about these centralised repositories. The dream of many technologists and futurists was a decentralised data system — a network where data ownership was democratised and spread across its users, rather than controlled by a handful of corporations.

Blockchain technology, with its decentralised ledgers and immutable records, emerged as a potential solution. New platforms started to experiment with decentralised clouds, where data was stored across multiple nodes, ensuring no single point of failure. This not only bolstered security but also gave users more control and ownership of their data. Smart contracts facilitated seamless, trust-less transactions in this environment, marking a revolutionary shift in how data could be stored and accessed.

The vision was grand: a global cloud free from the grips of monopolistic control, where every user was an equal stakeholder. However, the transition was far from smooth. Issues of scalability, energy consumption, and public understanding of such a paradigm stood as significant hurdles.

Amidst all the challenges and changes, one dream persisted: the idea of the global cloud as a universally accessible library. This dream was not just about storage but about knowledge dissemination. The global cloud had the potential to be the greatest educational tool humanity had ever seen.

Efforts were underway to digitise every book, article, and piece of art ever created, making them accessible to anyone with an internet connection. Projects like the Digital Public Library of America and Google Books aimed to make vast troves of information available to the public, regardless of their geographical location or financial status.

Moreover, this universal library was not static. It was constantly evolving, with users from around the world contributing to its expanse daily. Collaborative platforms allowed for real-time knowledge creation and sharing, breaking down traditional barriers in education and research.

The implications were profound. The universality of access meant that a child in a remote village had the same wealth of information at their fingertips as a student at a prestigious university. The global cloud, in its truest form, had the power to democratise knowledge like never before.

With the widespread adoption of the global cloud, the nature of information itself began to change. Previously, knowledge was often hoarded, either in the vaults of institutions or behind the paywalls of publishers. Now, the vast expanse of human understanding was at everyone's fingertips. But with this newfound accessibility came questions of ownership and authority.

In this new era, who owned information? The old structures, where authors and publishers held exclusive rights, began to be challenged. Open-source and community-driven projects came to the forefront, emphasising the collective creation and ownership of knowledge. Wikipedia, an early example, had set the tone, but now myriad platforms allowed experts and novices alike to contribute to the ever-expanding body of human understanding.

The concept of information "expiry" gained traction. Just as software could be updated in real-time, so too could pieces of information. Historical events, scientific theories, cultural nuances - all became fluid and subject to constant revision and enhancement. Some hailed this as the dawn of "living knowledge", while others expressed concerns about the potential for misinformation.

Parallel to the shifts in information ownership was a change in how history itself was documented. The global cloud, with its vast capacity and real-time update capabilities, became the de facto record keeper of human events. Gone were the days when events were recorded months or years after they transpired. Now, every tweet, post, or video became a part of the collective historical record.

This instantaneous documentation brought both opportunities and challenges. On the one hand, the nuances of events were captured with unprecedented detail. The voices of everyday people, not just the influential or powerful, found a place in the annals of history. On the other hand, the sheer volume of information made discerning the "truth" more challenging. Historians and analysts had to sift through terabytes of data, using advanced AI tools, to piece together coherent narratives.

Additionally, the permanence of digital records raised ethical concerns. Mistakes, once committed online, could not be undone. The concept of "right to be forgotten," where individuals could request their digital traces to be erased, became a hotly debated topic. Balancing historical integrity with individual privacy was a tightrope that societies worldwide grappled with.

As the capabilities of the global cloud expanded, many began to dream of its evolution into a fully decentralised system. Such a configuration would democratise data access further, eliminating central points of control or potential failure. This ideal system wouldn't be held hostage by corporate interests or governmental oversight, making it resilient against censorship or selective information suppression.

The blockchain technology, which had made waves in the financial sector decades earlier, emerged as a promising foundation for this vision. By ensuring data integrity without a central authority, blockchain-based decentralised data systems promised a transparent and incorruptible record of human knowledge. Every change, every addition to this knowledge base, would be permanently logged and verifiable by anyone.

Initial experiments in creating decentralised cloud structures faced challenges, especially in scalability and speed. Yet, as technology progressed, new solutions emerged that balanced decentralisation's ideals with the practical needs of vast data storage and quick access.

Parallel to technical developments was a cultural and philosophical movement advocating for unrestricted knowledge access. The dream was a library unlike any other in history: a universally accessible repository where anyone, irrespective of their location, background, or financial capability, could access the sum total of human understanding.

This wasn't just about reading materials. It encompassed all forms of knowledge - from academic lectures and research papers to artisan skills and oral histories from remote communities. The diversity of knowledge formats posed its challenges. How do you catalog a dance form or a culinary tradition? How do you ensure the context isn't lost when presenting indigenous wisdom?

Innovative solutions emerged. Augmented Reality (AR) and Virtual Reality (VR) experiences allowed users to immerse themselves in knowledge, be it walking through a historical event or learning a craft from a master halfway across the world. These immersive experiences, combined with advanced AI-driven translation tools, ensured that language and contextual barriers slowly diminished, making the dream of a universally accessible library inch closer to reality.

The Next Step - Pioneering Towards a Digital Utopia

Dawn of the 21st century brought with it a range of technological marvels, but few captured the imagination as vividly as augmented reality (AR). While virtual reality (VR) promised an escape to entirely digital realms, AR sought to merge the physical and virtual, enriching our everyday environment with a layer of digital data and interaction.

At its inception, AR was a clunky affair. Bulky headsets and slow rendering meant the augmented reality of the early days was a far cry from the seamless blending we dreamed of. But the potential was evident. Imagine looking at an old historical building and instantly seeing its history, architectural specifics, and anecdotes from the past. Or walking through a grocery store and having your dietary requirements or recipes visually overlaid on products as you pass by.

The initial challenges weren't just technical. There were also significant social hurdles. How would society react to people who seemed to be perpetually distracted, gazing at digital apparitions invisible to the non-augmented eye? And more importantly, how would our cognitive processes evolve with such constant multi-layered interaction?

With the rise of AR, VR, and the Global Cloud, our world had irrevocably changed. People now lived two lives: one in the real world and one in the digital. This duality brought with it a new set of societal norms and etiquettes. It wasn't just about not walking into a lamppost while engrossed in an AR experience; it was about understanding when to switch off, how to engage with others who might not be on the same digital platform, and respecting digital and physical boundaries.

In this increasingly connected age, personal space took on a new dimension. The concept of 'digital personal space' emerged. Just because you could send someone a holographic message or share an AR experience didn't mean you should, especially without permission. This new realm required a complete rethink of what privacy meant.

Moreover, the concept of 'presence' evolved. Being physically present in a location didn't guarantee your attention. People had to learn to navigate and prioritise these dual realities. New etiquettes were established, such as 'AR-free zones' in cafes or the gentle nudge of "IRL mode" prompts at family gatherings.

The educational sector saw a profound transformation. Traditional classrooms became obsolete, replaced by dynamic learning environments where history lessons took place on the battlegrounds of ancient wars and science lessons on the surface of Mars.

However, with all these advancements, there came pitfalls. The line between reality and the digital realm blurred for some, leading to psychological challenges. Digital addiction reached new heights, with individuals losing themselves in these alternate realities, sometimes preferring them to the bleakness or mundanity of their physical lives.

Yet, as with every major shift in society, humans adapted, evolved, and set boundaries. The promise of a digital utopia still beckoned, but it was clear that it would be a journey fraught with both wonder and caution.

In a world increasingly influenced by digital realms, the concept of identity underwent a profound transformation. No longer bound by physical limitations, individuals could craft personas in countless digital domains. These avatars, ranging from realistic to fantastical, became extensions of oneself, often revealing hidden desires, fears, or aspirations.

However, this freedom of expression also brought forward a dilemma. When presented with endless possibilities, what did it mean to be 'authentic'? A debate raged on about the true nature of self in the digital age. Some argued that their digital personas were their most genuine selves, free from societal judgments and constraints. Others felt it was but a curated, even deceptive, version of their identity.

The economic sector tapped into this evolving concept of identity. Companies emerged offering 'digital identity crafting' services, promising the perfect avatar, tailored online interactions, and even crafting entire digital histories. But this commodification of identity raised ethical concerns. If one could simply purchase an identity, was it genuine? Or was authenticity something intrinsically personal that couldn't be commercialised?

The malleability of identity in digital realms had profound implications on relationships and social dynamics. Virtual Reality became a popular venue for social interactions, from casual meet ups in breathtaking landscapes to profound bonding experiences in meticulously crafted scenarios.

Dating in the digital age saw transformations beyond just online matchmaking. Virtual dates became common, allowing couples to have dinner under the Northern Lights or stroll through recreated Renaissance-era streets without leaving their homes. Some even argued that these digital interactions allowed for deeper connections, as people were less bound by physical appearances and more focused on genuine conversations and shared experiences.

However, this shift wasn't without challenges. As much as technology allowed connections across vast distances, it also brought potential isolation. People grappled with the conundrum of having hundreds of virtual friends but feeling lonely in the physical world. The distinction between a 'digital friend' and a 'real-world friend' became blurrier, prompting many to question the very nature of friendship.

Family dynamics evolved. 'Digital family gatherings' became a norm, especially in an increasingly globalised world. These virtual reunions, while ensuring connectivity, also highlighted the irreplaceable warmth of physical presence. It was a poignant reminder that while technology could bridge many gaps, some human experiences remained deeply rooted in the tangible world.

As the world charged forth into this new digital frontier, not everyone was on board the ship. The digital divide, the gap between those who have access to technology and the internet and those who don't, widened exponentially. While urban centres transformed into high-tech hubs, rural areas in many parts of the world lagged, leading to a stark disparity in digital literacy and opportunities.

Children in remote villages, despite being of the same age, found themselves generations behind their urban counterparts in technological know-how. The divide wasn't just geographical; socio-economic factors played a colossal role. Those with the means adopted the latest AR and VR technologies, while the underprivileged had limited, if any, access.

/imagine A futuristic classroom with levitating desks, holographic displays, and floating orbs (representing AI). Children of diverse backgrounds engage with these AI entities, which adapt their forms to each student's learning style.

Governments and NGOs stepped in, initiating digital literacy campaigns, offering subsidised technology packs, and building infrastructure to connect the unconnected. However, they faced a multitude of challenges, from convincing traditional communities about the benefits of the digital age to addressing the high costs involved in setting up modern tech facilities in remote locations.

With such vast realms of virtual experiences, ethical questions inevitably arose. If one committed a crime in a virtual world, were they guilty in the real world? How did society judge morality when the lines between reality and simulation blurred?

Virtual worlds became spaces where people experimented with moral boundaries. Some saw it as a harmless sandbox, a place to vent and explore without real-world repercussions. However, others warned of the psychological effects. Acts in virtual worlds could desensitise individuals, making them more prone to replicating such behaviours in the physical realm.

Digital immortality was now within reach. With enough data and advanced algorithms, virtual avatars of deceased individuals could continue interacting with the living. This brought solace to some, providing a way to cope with grief. But it also raised ethical dilemmas. Was it right to 'resurrect' someone digitally? Did the digital self have rights?

The challenges of this era were manifold, and society often found itself scrambling to adapt. But adapt it did, continuously shaping and reshaping the code of ethics for the digital age. These guidelines served as the compass, ensuring humanity did not lose its essence while navigating the vast ocean of virtual possibilities.

In the early days of the internet, it was touted as the great equaliser, a realm where all were anonymous, and the traditional hierarchies didn't apply. However, as the virtual worlds grew more complex and intertwined with our physical existence, distinct societal structures began to emerge.

Virtual societies formed around common interests, ideologies, and even virtual geographies. With the development of the Metaverse – an expansive, interconnected digital universe – virtual nations and city-states sprouted. These entities had their own governance models, economic systems, and even virtual currencies.

Citizenship in these virtual nations wasn't bound by birth but by choice. Individuals could be citizens of multiple realms, each offering different experiences, rights, and responsibilities. Some were direct democracies where every member had a say in decision-making; others were technocracies ruled by those with the most advanced knowledge.

However, challenges arose. How were disputes between virtual nations settled? What happened when the economic system of one virtual state crashed? These challenges necessitated the creation of a Metaversal United Nations, a governing body aimed at ensuring peace and stability across the vast digital landscape.

The dream of a universal digital society was on the horizon. A world where every individual, regardless of their physical location, socio-economic status, or cultural background, could access the same wealth of information, opportunities, and experiences. But was it truly achievable?

As more and more individuals plugged into the digital realm, the physical world started seeing the effects. While virtual societies flourished, real-world cities grappled with depopulation. Nature started reclaiming spaces as more individuals chose the digital over the physical.

On the one hand, the environment benefited. With fewer people commuting or consuming physical goods, carbon footprints reduced, and wildlife thrived. But on the other, the very fabric of physical human interaction was at stake. Virtual hugs couldn't replace the warmth of a real embrace, and pixelated sunsets paled in comparison to the real thing.

A divide emerged between 'Naturalists' and 'Digitalists.' The former advocated for a balance, emphasising the importance of real-world experiences, while the latter believed in the superiority of the digital realm, where the only limits were those of imagination.

The universal digital society's dream was both promising and perilous. It held the potential to unite humanity in ways previously unimaginable but also threatened the essence of what it meant to be human.

In the vast expanse of the digital universe, the very notion of 'self' underwent a profound transformation. No longer confined by physical appearances, individuals could craft their digital personas in ways that best expressed their innermost selves. Avatars weren't mere visual representations but were deep manifestations of one's identity.

This fluidity of identity posed new questions about authenticity. Was your digital self more 'you' than your physical form? For many, the freedom to be who they truly felt they were inside, without the constraints of societal expectations, was liberating. For others, the constant reshaping of digital personas led to an identity crisis, where the lines between the real and the virtual blurred.

Simultaneously, new ethical concerns arose. With the ability to shape one's persona came the power to deceive. Fake avatars, catfishing, and virtual scams became rampant, prompting calls for a system of 'digital authenticity.' Debates raged over how to validate someone's true self in an environment built on the premise of limitless self-expression.

The digital utopia wasn't just a social experiment; it was an economic powerhouse. Virtual economies burgeoned, rivalling, and often surpassing their real-world counterparts. Virtual real estate sales broke records, digital art auctions went into the millions, and in-game currencies became as valuable as traditional fiat currencies.

However, this rapid economic growth wasn't without its pitfalls. Speculative bubbles formed, reminiscent of the dot-com boom and crash of the early 2000s. When a popular virtual city's real estate market collapsed, it wiped out billions in virtual wealth, leading to real-world ramifications for investors.

Central to these economic discussions was the role of cryptocurrency. As decentralised financial systems, cryptocurrencies were the backbone of many virtual economies. They enabled borderless transactions, ensuring that a user from any part of the world could participate in any virtual economy. Yet, their volatility and susceptibility to manipulation remained major concerns.

Governments struggled to regulate these new economic entities. How does one tax a virtual transaction? How does one prevent money laundering in the digital realm? The challenges were manifold, but they also presented opportunities for reinventing the very foundations of global economic systems.

The classrooms of yore, with their chalkboards and wooden desks, seemed a distant memory. In the digital utopia, learning spaces were redefined, transcending physical boundaries. These new-age classrooms were not confined to four walls but stretched across vast virtual terrains, accessible to anyone with a digital connection.

Educational institutions adopted augmented reality (AR) and virtual reality (VR) to create immersive learning experiences. Students could now explore the ruins of ancient Rome, dive deep into the Mariana Trench, or even walk on the surface of Mars - all from the comfort of their homes. The tactile and sensory experiences these technologies provided made learning more engaging and memorable.

With the global accessibility of digital education platforms, knowledge became democratised. A child in a remote village in Africa could attend the same class as someone in bustling New York City. This led to a profound cultural exchange, where students were not just learning academic concepts but also gaining insights into diverse ways of life from peers across the globe.

However, the digitalisation of education wasn't devoid of challenges. While technology bridged many gaps, it also highlighted the digital divide – the gulf between those who had access to digital tools and those who didn't. Ensuring equitable access to quality digital education became a focal point of global discourse.

Relationships, the very fabric of human society, underwent significant transformation in the digital realm. No longer limited by geographical constraints, people formed bonds with individuals from distant corners of the world. These connections, often deep and meaningful, challenged traditional notions of relationships based on physical proximity.

Digital platforms gave birth to new forms of expression. Virtual hugs, digital gifts, and avatar dances became standard ways of conveying emotions. In this vast digital landscape, even the concept of romance evolved. Virtual dates at sunset beaches or atop digital skyscrapers became the norm, with couples celebrating 'metaversaries' – anniversaries of when they first met in the virtual world.

Yet, the depth of these virtual connections also raised concerns. Mental health professionals debated the impact of digital relationships on the human psyche. Did these relationships, no matter how profound, fulfill the innate human need for physical touch and connection? Or were they leading to a new form of isolation, where one could be surrounded by a plethora of virtual friends yet feel profoundly alone?

The journey through the digital utopia continued, challenging long-held beliefs and norms, reshaping the way humanity perceived itself and the world around. As the story unfolds, we turn our attention to governance and leadership in this brave new world.

Holographic Projections

In the latter half of the 20th century, humanity took its first tentative steps into a world once confined to the realm of science fiction: holography. The inception of holography traces back to physicist Dennis Gabor's groundbreaking work in the 1940s, for which he was awarded the Nobel Prize. This three-dimensional imaging technique utilised laser light interference to project volumetric pictures suspended in space, seemingly defying the laws of physics.

Over the subsequent decades, the field of holography underwent numerous evolutions, each iteration making the technology more precise and accessible. By the dawn of the 21st century, rudimentary holograms, once a novelty in select laboratories, found their way into pop culture, with iconic cinematic moments from films like "Star Wars" bringing the idea to the public eye.

However, the real game-changer came when corporations and tech startups realised the potential of holography. Companies ranging from tech giants to niche entertainment startups began pouring investments into research and development, refining the technology. Before long, holographic concerts began to emerge, with late artists seemingly "resurrected" on stage, delivering performances to awe-struck audiences. Moreover, the educational sector experienced a paradigm shift. Imagine history lessons where students could witness a life-sized holographic recreation of the Gettysburg Address or scientific lectures enhanced with three-dimensional holographic molecules floating amongst the students.

The next monumental leap in holography came with its fusion with augmented reality (AR). With AR's capacity to overlay virtual elements onto the real world through devices like smart glasses or mobile screens, it was only logical to introduce volumetric, three-dimensional holographs into this mix.

This convergence led to revolutionary applications. Now, users could interact with holograms in their living spaces, transforming their surroundings into dynamic canvases. Imagine turning one's lounge into the lunar surface and walking alongside the Apollo 11 astronauts or watching as a holographic lion sauntered through the backyard.

Development platforms and user-friendly software became accessible, empowering creators worldwide. From independent artists to major tech enterprises, a flurry of apps and experiences flooded the market. These platforms, intuitive in design, enabled even those with limited technical know-how to craft intricate holographic scenes and share them with a global audience.

However, the merging of AR and holography wasn't without its challenges. Perfecting the interactivity, ensuring the holograms reacted believably to the physical world's nuances, became the new frontier. But with every problem came innovative solutions, with AI playing a pivotal role in enhancing the believability and responsiveness of these holographic projections.

As we delve deeper into the chapter, we will explore the challenges holography faced, its utility beyond mere entertainment, and the ethical implications of a world where the lines between the real and the virtual start to blur.

With every technological advancement, there are hurdles to overcome, and the rise of holography was no exception. As the technology grew more pervasive, numerous challenges emerged, both technical and socio-cultural.

On the technical front, producing high-resolution, lifelike holograms that could be viewed from multiple angles without distortion proved to be a significant challenge. Early holograms often suffered from glitches, transparency issues, and a limited field of view. Brightness and visibility in various lighting conditions also became a concern. And as the demand for interactive holograms surged, ensuring smooth real-time rendering and accurate depth perception was paramount.

Additionally, there were issues concerning power consumption and device miniaturisation. Powering high-definition holograms required significant energy, and in an age where mobility and wireless tech were the norms, bulky setups with wired connections were deemed archaic.

However, the tech world was quick to respond. Innovations in photonics and nanotechnology paved the way for more efficient, compact projectors. Advanced algorithms, powered by the surge in AI capabilities, refined depth perception and interactivity. Companies collaborated, merging various tech solutions – from AI-driven rendering techniques to advanced sensors – crafting a more immersive and real holographic experience.

But beyond the technical lay socio-cultural challenges. In a world where holographic projections could look and feel real, the risk of counterfeit recreations became genuine. The boundaries between what was real and what was virtually crafted grew porous. There were cases of unsuspecting individuals being deceived by holographic recreations of real-world items, leading to concerns about the misuse of the technology.

The presence of life-sized virtual beings posed new questions about privacy. With holographic tech's ability to recreate someone's likeness in a three-dimensional space, the threat of voyeuristic tendencies, identity theft, and unauthorised recreations became more pronounced.

Governments, tech giants, and civil society began working in tandem to navigate these uncharted waters. Regulations emerged to safeguard individuals from unauthorised recreations and to clamp down on counterfeit holographic products. And with these measures in place, society began to truly harness holography's benefits.

As holography matured, its applications transcended mere entertainment. Industries across the spectrum began leveraging this groundbreaking tech to transform their operations.

In the realm of medicine, surgeons started utilising holographic displays to get a comprehensive three-dimensional view of the human anatomy. Such detailed visuals proved invaluable during intricate procedures, allowing for more precision and reducing potential risks. Medical students, too, benefited, as they could now study the human body like never before, dissecting virtual patients without the limitations of traditional methods.

The architectural world underwent a revolution of its own. Gone were the days of two-dimensional blueprints; architects could now visualise entire structures in holographic 3D, making real-time modifications and collaborating with teams across the globe. Clients could embark on virtual tours of yet-to-be-constructed buildings, offering feedback and ensuring the final product was in line with their vision.

Entertainment, too, took a giant leap. While holographic concerts were the initial rage, the growth of holographic theatres transformed the cinematic experience. Audiences could now be amidst the action, with characters and scenes unfolding all around them. This immersive format gave filmmakers a brand-new canvas, leading to innovative storytelling methods.

Remote collaboration, a necessity in an increasingly globalised world, became more seamless. Board meetings, academic lectures, and even casual catch-ups were enriched with lifelike holographic avatars, reducing the distance between participants and fostering a sense of presence.

As holography's footprint expanded, society began to witness its transformative potential, not just as a tool for spectacle but as a means to enrich, educate, and empower.

The horizon of holography is vast and ever-evolving, with the technology's potential limited only by human imagination. As we stand on the cusp of this new era, several forward-looking trends and speculations shape our collective vision for what lies ahead.

The evolution of the internet has been nothing short of spectacular. From rudimentary text-based sites to the rich multimedia platforms of today, our digital journey has been transformative. And now, holography promises to take this journey to its next logical step - a truly immersive internet.

Imagine a digital realm where websites aren't just pages but entire three-dimensional spaces. E-commerce sites where you can walk through virtual aisles, examining products from every angle. Social media platforms where avatars of friends and family interact in a shared virtual space. Museums where art and history come alive, and you can take guided tours led by lifelike holographic guides. The possibilities are endless.

As the bandwidth and infrastructure of the global internet evolve, this dream inches closer to reality. Pioneering platforms are already offering glimpses of this future, and as they gain traction, our very understanding of 'browsing the web' is set to undergo a paradigm shift.

This brave new world won't be without its challenges. The fusion of the virtual and real through holography raises ethical questions that society will need to grapple with. If our likeness can be recreated and deployed in digital spaces without our consent, what does that mean for personal agency and identity? When virtual representations can impact real-world reputations, how do we ensure fairness and justice?

Another concern will be the blurring of reality and fiction. As holographic recreations become more realistic, distinguishing between what's real and what's virtual could become challenging, especially for younger generations who grow up in a world where such technology is ubiquitous.

The immersive internet could potentially exacerbate issues like digital addiction. When virtual spaces feel as real and compelling as physical ones, the temptation to spend more time in them might be overwhelming for some. Mental health

/imagine A massive, intricately designed AI-driven loom, weaving together threads of different colors and textures. Each thread represents different facets of culture: art, music, media. The woven tapestry showcases iconic cultural symbols from around the world, illustrating how AI threads together global cultures.

professionals and technologists will need to work together to understand and mitigate such challenges.

One of the most exciting prospects of holographic technology is the potential for a universally accessible library —a global repository where knowledge isn't just stored but experienced. Students worldwide could delve into detailed holographic lessons, making education more engaging and accessible. Historical events could be recreated, allowing people to 'witness' moments of the past, making learning more immersive and memorable.

This vision aligns with the broader aspiration of many tech pioneers: to democratise access to knowledge and experiences. With the right policies and infrastructure investments, the holographic revolution could play a pivotal role in bridging global educational gaps and creating a more informed and interconnected world.

As holography continues to shape our world, its impact will be felt across every facet of human endeavour. While the challenges are real, so are the opportunities. In the coming decades, holography might not just change the way we see the world but also how we understand and engage with it.

Entertainment, especially cinema and music, often come to mind when thinking about holography. However, the applications of holography extend well beyond these realms. In the medical field, holographic displays provide surgeons with 3D visualisations of complex procedures, allowing them to navigate intricate surgeries with greater precision. By overlaying holographic images onto a patient's body, surgeons get a real-time guide, drastically reducing risks and enhancing outcomes.

In the world of architecture and construction, holography has transformed the design phase. Architects can now create full-scale holographic models of their projects, enabling clients to "walk through" a building before a single brick is laid. This interactive approach helps in refining designs, anticipating problems, and ensuring that the final structure aligns perfectly with the vision.

Moreover, in fields like archaeology and palaeontology, holograms recreate historical sites or extinct creatures, offering researchers a tangible look at the past. These lifelike models are invaluable in understanding historical contexts and drawing insights that were previously impossible.

The COVID-19 pandemic underscored the importance of remote collaboration. While tools like video conferencing played a vital role, holography has the potential to redefine remote interactions. With the ability to project lifelike avatars of individuals into meeting rooms, holography offers a more immersive and interactive experience than flat screens.

Companies are beginning to harness this potential, especially in sectors where visual collaboration is crucial. From brainstorming sessions in advertising agencies to detailed product design discussions in tech firms, holographic meetings are fast becoming a reality. This not only enhances productivity but also reduces the need for travel, contributing to a greener planet.

Furthermore, cultural and familial connections severed by distance can be rekindled. Imagine grandparents being able to project themselves into their grandchildren's living rooms, sharing stories and experiences as if they were physically present. The emotional connect this technology can foster is truly groundbreaking.

The entertainment industry has been quick to grasp the potential of holography. From resurrecting legendary artists for concerts to creating entirely holographic performances, the boundaries of what's possible are continuously expanding.

Holographic theatres, a concept once restricted to science fiction, are emerging in major cities. These venues, equipped with state-of-the-art holographic projection systems, offer audiences an unparalleled visual treat. Traditional plays acquire a new dimension, with characters and scenes becoming more dynamic. Fantastical tales, which were once challenging to stage, can now be brought to life in all their glory.

Similarly, events like product launches, fashion shows, and art exhibitions are leveraging holography to offer richer experiences. Product demos can be more interactive, with devices being showcased in 360-degree detail. Fashion shows can have models walking beside their holographic counterparts, presenting the past, present, and future of design on a single runway.

While purists may argue that holography takes away from the "real" experience, there's no denying that it adds a layer of magic, making each event memorable. As the technology matures and becomes more accessible, holographic theatres and events are set to become the norm, reshaping the entertainment landscape.

As with any technological evolution, it's difficult to predict with certainty where holography will lead us, but the horizons seem boundless. Current trajectories and research hint at some intriguing possibilities. For starters, the fidelity and resolution of holograms will undoubtedly improve, allowing for even more lifelike and immersive experiences.

Personal holography might become commonplace. Imagine a future where personal devices, like our smartphones today, can project high-definition holograms. Communication would be revolutionised once more, with holographic video calls becoming the norm. It's not just about seeing someone in 2D on a screen, but having their 3D representation right in front of you.

On a grander scale, the convergence of AI and holography could lead to responsive holographic entities that can interact with users, understand context, and provide real-time feedback. These entities could serve multiple roles, from educators to personal health trainers, to interactive storytellers for children.

Moreover, as we tread deeper into the realms of virtual reality and augmented reality, holography could serve as the bridge that merges these two worlds, delivering experiences that are neither entirely real nor entirely virtual, but something uniquely in between.

The concept of a 'Metaverse'—an expansive, immersive virtual universe—is gaining traction. Holography might be the key to unlocking its true potential. Rather than wearing bulky VR headsets or staring at screens, holographic projections could bring the virtual world to our living rooms.

Shopping could be transformed. Instead of scrolling through images, users could interact with holographic versions of products. Online learning could be revolutionised with virtual classrooms where students and teachers, although miles apart, feel like they're in the same room.

Furthermore, imagine social media platforms where users can send holographic statuses or memories, making interactions more vivid and personal. The lines between the physical and digital worlds would blur, crafting an internet experience that's more visceral than ever before.

But beyond the applications, this could change the fundamental way we perceive the internet—not just as a vast repository of information but as a living, breathing entity capable of coming to us, interacting with us, and becoming a part of our daily lives in ways we've never imagined.

However, this utopia isn't without its challenges. As the virtual and real worlds merge, a plethora of ethical concerns emerge. With lifelike holograms, how do we determine the real from the fake? Deepfakes, already a concern with 2D video, could evolve into something even more deceptive and damaging.

Privacy is another massive concern. If our personal devices emit holographic projections, what's stopping unauthorised entities from accessing and projecting our private moments? The very tools meant to connect us might end up becoming tools of surveillance.

As holograms become more interactive and AI-driven, there's a risk of them becoming too influential, particularly on impressionable minds. Children growing up with responsive holographic companions might struggle to differentiate between genuine human interactions and AI-driven ones.

Regulations will inevitably have to evolve, with stringent safeguards ensuring that the wonder of holography isn't overshadowed by potential misuse. The future is exciting, but as with all things, it comes with its set of challenges that we must prepare for.

Since its inception, holography has fascinated and captivated the human imagination. The dream of replicating reality, creating lifelike 3D images suspended in mid-air, has its roots in ancient history. Shadows on cave walls and illusions created by early optics teased at this concept. But it wasn't until the 20th century that the science of holography began in earnest.

The term "holography" originates from the Greek words "holos" (whole) and "graphé" (writing), which precisely encapsulates the essence of the technique: capturing the entirety of a light field. The 1960s saw the first practical demonstrations of laser-based holography by Dr. Dennis Gabor, who later earned the Nobel Prize for his groundbreaking work. Since those early days, holography has come a long way, evolving from rudimentary laser setups producing static images to the dynamic, high-resolution displays we see today.

The initial appeal of holography was primarily academic, with universities and research institutions at the forefront of its exploration. However, the entertainment industry quickly saw its potential. The first holographic art exhibitions in the 1970s showcased the novelty of 3D imaging, and soon after, the music industry began experimenting with holographic album covers, adding a touch of futuristic flair.

But the real game-changer was the adoption of holography by the broader tech industry. As display technology advanced and miniaturisation became possible, tech giants began incorporating holographic elements into their products. The early 2000s witnessed the unveiling of holographic storage devices, promising unparalleled data densities. Moreover, the world watched in astonishment as deceased artist Tupac Shakur was "resurrected" as a hologram at a music festival, marking a turning point in public awareness of the technology's potential.

The Tupac performance was merely the tip of the iceberg. Soon, holography began making inroads into diverse sectors. The medical field began experimenting with holographic imaging, offering surgeons a 3D perspective during intricate procedures. Educational institutions started to see the potential for holographic lectures, where historical figures or complex biological processes could be visualised in full 3D.

Pop stars, from Michael Jackson to Whitney Houston, had posthumous performances, thrilling fans and offering a new kind of concert experience. Furthermore, businesses began leveraging holography for teleconferencing, creating the illusion of physical presence and bridging geographical divides.

In essence, the once-elusive dream of holography became an integral part of our everyday lives. From the entertainment we consume to the way we learn and communicate, holograms have transformed the texture of our interactions, providing depth, both literally and metaphorically, to our experiences.

Augmented Reality (AR) and holography, though distinct, share a kindred spirit. Both aim to enhance the real world by layering additional information or experiences on top of it. As technological barriers diminished, a natural fusion of these two domains began to manifest.

Early AR implementations, like Google Glass, provided a heads-up display overlaying digital information onto the user's field of view. Simultaneously, holographic displays aimed to project 3D images into real space. The convergence seemed inevitable. Why settle for flat overlays when you could have dynamic, 3D holographic augmentations?

Soon, companies at the forefront of AR tech started integrating holographic displays into their products. This hybrid approach presented users with richer, more immersive experiences. Walking down the street, one could see holographic arrows guiding them to their destination or have a full-size 3D model of a product they're considering purchasing appear before them.

The next challenge was interaction. It's one thing to see a hologram; it's another to interact with it as you would a tangible object. Advances in sensors and machine learning enabled devices to understand user gestures and movements. Swiping, grabbing, pushing – these natural motions were now the language of holographic AR interactions.

The implications were profound. Architects could modify 3D holographic blueprints in real-time using their hands. Students could dissect holographic animals, delving into layers, systems, and structures. Gamers could physically interact with virtual characters and objects, breaking the boundary between the game world and reality.

As with any transformative technology, democratisation was the final frontier. Major tech companies began releasing SDKs (Software Development Kits) and platforms, empowering developers to craft their own holographic AR experiences. This wave of democratisation gave rise to an explosion of applications, from indie games to educational tools to art installations.

This fusion of AR and holography marked a paradigm shift. No longer were these domains the purview of tech giants and specialised labs. Everyone, from the solo developer to the classroom teacher, had the tools to create, innovate, and reshape the fabric of reality itself.

As with any technological advancement, the journey of holography was not without its roadblocks. The primary challenge was achieving true, high-resolution, 3D holograms that could be viewed from any angle without the need for special glasses or external devices. Early holograms suffered from limited viewing angles and required precise lighting conditions to be viewed correctly.

Another significant hurdle was the vast computational power required to generate and project dynamic holograms in real-time. Traditional 2D displays utilise pixels, but holograms require a more complex unit: the "hogel," or holographic pixel. Calculating the interference pattern for each hogel in real-time presented a computational challenge that demanded the creation of specialised chips and software optimisation techniques.

Battery life and energy consumption were also critical concerns, especially for portable devices. Projecting holograms consumes significant energy, and without advances in battery technology and energy-efficient projection techniques, the dream of mobile holographic displays seemed distant.

While the technological challenges were daunting, the socio-cultural implications of holography presented equally complex problems. The ability to project life-sized, realistic holograms raised profound questions about identity, presence, and reality.

For instance, the posthumous holographic performances of celebrities sparked debates about consent, legacy, and the ethics of 'resurrecting' the dead for commercial gain. Moreover, the possibility of creating holographic replicas of living individuals led to concerns about impersonation, identity theft, and privacy. In a world where a convincing holographic double could be created, how would society ensure authenticity and trust in interpersonal interactions?

Privacy became a paramount concern. With holographic technology enabling hyper-realistic projections, the potential for misuse was evident. Imagine scenarios where individuals could spy on others using holographic avatars or gather sensitive information without being physically present.

The proliferation of holographic tech also saw a rise in voyeuristic tendencies. With the capability to project and view realistic holograms, boundaries began blurring. The "window into someone else's life" became literal, as people started projecting their lives for others to view. This led to a necessary debate about consent, boundaries, and the ethics of viewing versus experiencing reality.

While the entertainment value of holograms was evident and mesmerising, the real potential of holography lay in its practical applications across diverse fields. Medicine was one of the first domains to harness the potential of holography fully. Surgeons began using holographic displays to visualise complex procedures, turning intricate surgeries

/imagine A modern living room setting. On one side, a family is engaged in traditional activities, reading, playing, conversing. On the other, the same family interacts seamlessly with transparent AI entities, whether it's through holographic games, AI-driven home assistants, or virtual pets. This duality captures the integration of AI in everyday lives.

183

into more manageable tasks with a 3D perspective. Imagine a cardiologist viewing a real-time holographic projection of a beating heart, making precise interventions with unprecedented clarity.

In the realm of architecture and urban planning, holograms transformed the way designs were conceptualised and presented. Architects could now walk clients through a life-sized holographic model of a building, tweaking designs in real-time based on feedback. This tactile, immersive approach revolutionised client-architect interactions, fostering better understanding and collaboration.

The corporate world wasn't left behind in the holographic revolution. As telecommuting and remote work became the norm, the limitations of 2D video conferencing became evident. Enter holographic conferencing. Now, colleagues could feel as if they were sitting across the same table, discussing, brainstorming, and collaborating, irrespective of the physical miles between them. This sense of presence, of 'being there,' bridged the emotional and psychological gaps that remote work often engendered.

Entertainment venues underwent a metamorphosis with the advent of holography. Traditional theatres began incorporating holographic elements, turning plays and performances into immersive experiences. Concerts were no longer restricted by the physical presence of artists. A singer could perform live in New York and have their holographic counterpart enthralling audiences in Tokyo simultaneously.

Such holographic events became a unique blend of live performance and technological marvel, offering audiences an experience that was both novel and nostalgically authentic.

The journey of holography, from its nascent stages to its revolutionary applications, has been nothing short of spectacular. But like any technological arc, the trajectory of holography also points to future possibilities, many of which remain in the realms of science fiction – for now.

One of the most anticipated advancements is the integration of haptic feedback with holographic projections. Imagine not only seeing a holographic apple but also 'feeling' it, experiencing its weight, texture, and even temperature. Such advancements would usher in a new era of virtual interactions, where the line between the digital and the physical becomes almost indistinguishable.

Another realm of possibility lies in the miniaturisation of holographic projectors. In a world where wearable tech is becoming ubiquitous, the dream of personal, wearable holographic projectors doesn't seem too far-fetched. This could redefine personal communication, where a call to a loved one is no longer confined to a screen but takes the form of their life-sized holographic projection right beside you.

The potential integration of quantum computing with holography is also a tantalising prospect. Quantum computers, with their unparalleled processing capabilities, could render large-scale, complex holograms in real-time, opening doors to applications we haven't even envisioned yet.

The evolution of the internet has been from text-based pages to rich multimedia experiences. With the advancements in holography, the next leap could be towards a truly immersive internet, where websites transform into interactive 3D spaces, and online shopping involves walking through virtual stores, examining products as holograms.

Online education would see a transformation, with classrooms becoming 3D interactive spaces, enabling students from around the world to 'sit' together and learn in a collaborative environment. Virtual tourism could become a widespread phenomenon, with individuals exploring landmarks, museums, and even natural wonders as holographic recreations.

While the potential of holography paints a rosy picture, it's imperative to consider the ethical ramifications of such a blended world. With the lines between reality and virtuality blurring, issues of truth, representation, and authenticity will come to the fore.

Would seeing be believing in a world populated with holograms? The possibilities for misinformation and manipulation are profound. Moreover, the idea of living in a world where one's perception is constantly augmented by holography raises concerns about the nature of experience, authenticity, and even human connection.

Furthermore, as holographic content becomes more mainstream, who gets to control, produce, and distribute it? Questions about the monopolisation of the holographic medium, its accessibility, and its potential as a tool for propaganda or social control become critical.

As with all technological advancements, the future of holography promises a mix of wonders and challenges. But one thing is clear: holography stands poised to reshape our reality, and how we navigate this new landscape will determine its legacy.

As holographic technology grows more sophisticated, a pressing concern is the rights associated with reproductions. For instance, when a deceased celebrity is "resurrected" for a concert or event, who truly has the rights to their holographic likeness? Beyond the realm of celebrities, what happens when everyday individuals find their images replicated without consent? Establishing clear guidelines around permissions and rights becomes essential in a world where one's likeness can be replicated with precision.

An increasing reliance on holographic interactions could create a societal divide between what is considered "real" and what is "virtual." With experiences becoming so lifelike, there is a risk that individuals may prioritise holographic interactions over real-life ones. This could lead to challenges in mental health, with people feeling more isolated despite being more "connected."

Moreover, how will the human brain, inherently wired to distinguish between the tangible and the intangible, react to prolonged exposure to a world where the two are indistinguishable? There might be unforeseen psychological implications that need to be considered and studied.

While holography offers an exceptional tool for education and the preservation of history, it also poses the risk of rewriting or altering it. For instance, historical events, when represented through holograms, could be modified, leading to a distorted understanding of our past. The ethical concerns here are vast – from who gets to decide the representation of historical figures to the danger of erasing uncomfortable parts of our history for a more sanitised version.

The issue of consent takes on a new dimension in the realm of holography. Imagine a future where personalised advertising is not just on screens but involves holographic projections tailored for individuals in public spaces. Or consider a world where personal memories can be played back as holographic projections. Who would have access to

/imagine A bridge merging two islands, representing the two learning types, with traffic (data) flowing seamlessly between them.

these? And how would consent be obtained, especially when dealing with personal and intimate memories?

For all the ethical challenges that holography presents, the onus lies with creators, policymakers, and users to navigate this landscape responsibly. This involves not just the establishment of clear legal frameworks but also fostering a culture of ethical holographic creation and consumption.

Educational institutions can play a pivotal role by incorporating ethics into curricula related to holographic design and application. Public discourse, open debates, and forums can provide platforms for diverse voices to discuss and shape the future direction of this technology.

While the allure of holography lies in its ability to create lifelike, immersive experiences, it's essential to remember that its true power lies in augmenting our reality, not replacing it. Balancing the marvels of the virtual with the grounding of the real will be the challenge and opportunity of the coming age.

As with every revolutionary technology, the horizon for holography is boundless. Each passing day ushers in innovations that push the envelope of what's possible. If the last decade was about refining and popularising holography, the next might very well be about redefining our reality with it.

Some of the immediate advancements on the horizon involve increasing the resolution and realism of holograms. Imagine holographic projections so crisp and lifelike that they are indistinguishable from reality. There are also strides being made in eliminating the need for specialised glasses or viewing angles to perceive holograms.

Another aspiration is the creation of interactive holograms, which are more sentient and reactive. Just beyond that vision lies the prospect of tactile holograms – projections you can touch and feel. Research in ultrasonic waves and targeted air pressure changes might soon make it possible to "feel" the warmth of a holographic fire or the cool splash of a virtual waterfall.

Furthermore, the world waits with bated breath for the invention of portable holography. The day when our smartphones or wristwatches can project a 3D holographic video call or a game is not too distant.

As we peer further into the future, one of the most tantalising prospects is the transformation of the internet into a fully immersive holographic space. Imagine logging onto a website and instead of viewing it on a screen, stepping into it as a 3D environment. E-commerce sites could allow you to walk through virtual aisles, pick up products, and examine them as if you were in a brick-and-mortar store. Social media would evolve from posts and images to immersive experiences shared in real-time with friends from around the world.

Museums and educational sites could offer holographic tours, allowing students to walk with dinosaurs, fly through the solar system, or stand in the middle of historical events. The possibilities are only limited by imagination.

But as the lines between the virtual and the real blur, new ethical challenges emerge. One of the most pressing is the concept of truth in a world where seeing is no longer believing. With the potential for realistic holographic manipulations, the age-old adage of "trust but verify" takes on new meaning.

There's also the matter of personal identity. If one can project any version of oneself – or indeed, someone else – into the holographic space, what does that mean for personal authenticity? What are the implications for personal relations, trust, and even crime?

Moreover, with the omnipresence of holographic projections, there's a potential risk of over-saturation. Just as today we grapple with screen addiction and digital detoxes, tomorrow's challenge might be finding genuine, unaltered moments amidst a sea of projections.

It's evident that as holography continues to meld with our daily lives, it brings with it a host of challenges and opportunities. And as with every transformative technology, it will be up to us to navigate its use responsibly, ensuring that it enhances rather than diminishes the human experience.

Exploring the Deep Universe

In the silent vastness of the cosmos, a revolution is unfolding. As we progressed into the 21st century, the rise of advanced space telescopes changed our perspective on the universe. Instruments like the James Webb Space Telescope, successors to the legendary Hubble, became our eyes into the deep corners of the cosmos, revealing galaxies, stars, and exoplanets in more detail than ever imagined. But while these tools extended our sight, it was the computational prowess of artificial intelligence that extended our understanding.

AI models began to analyse the petabytes of cosmic data we accumulated, spotting patterns and anomalies faster than any human or traditional computer model could. This amalgamation of optics and AI led to a clearer understanding of phenomena such as dark matter, black holes, and even the nascent stages of galaxy formation.

However, more than just stars and galaxies, one of the age-old questions in cosmology is the existence of extraterrestrial life. With advancements in technology, the hunt intensified. AI-driven analysis of explanatory atmospheres provided hints about potentially habitable planets. By analysing the light spectrum, we could gauge the composition of these far-off atmospheres, searching for signs of life or at least the conditions ripe for its evolution.

Parallel to our upward gaze, humanity's curiosity also drove us to the mysterious depths of our own planet. The oceans, covering over 70% of the Earth's surface, remained largely enigmatic, with vast portions still unexplored. But as the 21st century marched on, technological advancements in deep-sea exploration began to unravel the secrets held within the abyss.

Submersibles equipped with state-of-the-art sensors and cameras started venturing deeper and for longer durations. These expeditions revealed breathtaking landscapes, towering underwater mountains, sprawling trenches, and hydrothermal vents spewing minerals. With every dive, new species, previously unknown to science, were discovered. These ecosystems, isolated for millions of years, provided insights into life's adaptability and resilience.

The potential of the deep sea isn't just biological. Beneath the seabed lies an abundance of resources—rare minerals and metals essential for our technologically driven society. As we began to understand this underwater bounty, discussions about sustainable and responsible mining practices emerged, emphasising the need to balance technological advancement with ecological preservation.

As the narrative unfolds, these frontiers, both the vast expanse of the universe and the deep blue oceans, illustrate humanity's insatiable thirst for knowledge and exploration. The subsequent sections will delve into the equally mysterious realms of the human mind, the uncharted digital landscapes, and the very fabric of our reality.

The human brain, a web of nearly 100 billion neurons, is often considered one of the most intricate structures in the universe. For centuries, philosophers, scientists, and thinkers have pondered over the nuances of consciousness, emotions, and cognition. But the 21st century became a transformative era for neuroscience and our understanding of the human psyche.

Advancements in neuroimaging techniques, like real-time fMRI and PET scans, offered glimpses into the brain's active regions during various tasks, thoughts, and emotions. Machine learning algorithms trained on vast datasets began to predict behavioural patterns, offering novel insights into psychiatric disorders and their potential treatments. Deep Brain Stimulation (DBS) and similar technologies not only treated conditions like Parkinson's but also opened doors to potentially enhancing human cognitive capabilities.

However, the most audacious project was the neural mapping of the entire brain. AI-assisted technologies sought to chart every synapse, creating a comprehensive 'connectome' of the human mind. This endeavour provided profound insights into our memories, dreams, and even the nature of consciousness itself. Philosophical debates arose around these findings, pushing society to confront the very essence of what it means to be human.

While we ventured deep into space, oceans, and our minds, another frontier was rapidly expanding: the digital realm. With the progression of virtual reality, augmented reality, and the metaverse, the lines between the physical and the digital began to blur.

Virtual worlds became spaces for social interaction, commerce, and creativity. Massive virtual cities were erected, with their economies, cultures, and governance structures. AI-driven avatars interacted seamlessly with humans, making the virtual experience indistinguishable from the real. These digital landscapes became sanctuaries for expressions, offering people a chance to lead alternative lives, unburdened by physical limitations.

But these worlds were not without challenges. Digital real estate booms, data rights, and the concept of virtual citizenship became contentious topics. The nature of reality became a philosophical quandary. If one could feel, earn, love, and live in the digital space, what defined reality? With the metaverse's growth, these questions grew in significance, prompting societal, ethical, and legal debates about our digital existence.

As the chronicle continues, the subsequent segments will probe the boundaries of simulated realities, quantum realms, and the interplay of biology with technology, exploring the myriad paths humanity might tread in the quest for knowledge and existence.

As mankind delved deeper into the subatomic world, a universe of possibilities, both bizarre and enchanting, unfurled. Quantum mechanics, once an arcane branch of physics, took center stage in this epoch. Our elementary understanding of atoms and particles was replaced by a cloud of probabilities and entanglements, challenging the classical physics foundations.

Quantum computing, with its promise of computational prowess unparalleled by classical computers, reshaped industries. Problems once deemed unsolvable due to their sheer computational requirements became tractable. Cryptographic systems, the bedrock of digital security, had to be reimagined as quantum algorithms could potentially crack them. However, the quantum realm wasn't just about raw computational power; it brought with it the intriguing world of superpositions, where particles existed in multiple states simultaneously, and entanglements, which hinted at a deep-seated non-locality in nature.

Scientific endeavours began aiming to harness these oddities. Quantum teleportation, initially a theoretical construct, became a reality, even if in its infancy. Researchers discussed the possibilities of quantum networks, a new kind of internet that would be faster and inherently more secure due to the principles of quantum mechanics.

A parallel revolution was brewing in the fields of biology and technology. Instead of seeing them as distinct domains, visionaries started perceiving them as two sides of the same coin. Biological processes began to be understood in computational terms, while machines started integrating biological components to enhance their functions.

This blurring of boundaries led to radical innovations. Bio-computers, which used DNA strands and biological molecules to perform computations, were developed. These organic machines boasted of energy efficiency far surpassing their silicon counterparts. On the flip side, humans began augmenting their bodies with technology. Bionic limbs, equipped with sensory feedback, became commonplace. Neural implants bridged gaps in damaged neural networks, restoring lost functions and, in some cases, augmenting capabilities.

However, as with every innovation, ethical questions arose. What did it mean to be human in an age where the biological and the artificial were indistinguishably melded? As lines blurred and realms once thought distinct converged,

/imagine A monochrome scene of a bustling 20th-century city, gradually transitioning into vibrant colors towards the modern era. At the intersection of the two times, a figure stands, holding a lantern that emits binary codes instead of light, symbolizing the dawning age of artificial intelligence.

society stood at the crossroads, reflecting on the implications of its own creations.

The ensuing sections will dive into the societal responses to these profound shifts, exploring the challenges, opportunities, and philosophical conundrums they posed.

The intersection of quantum advances and the bio-technological fusion opened up numerous benefits for society, but it equally posed several ethical challenges. The very nature of blending the organic and inorganic, the biological and the computational, blurred lines and led to questions that humanity had never previously grappled with.

Take, for instance, the realm of enhanced humans. As bionic limbs and neural implants became sophisticated, there was a rise in "elective enhancements" – individuals choosing to replace perfectly healthy body parts with technologically superior alternatives. This posed significant social dilemmas. Would these enhanced humans still be considered entirely human, or were they transcending into a post-human phase? Furthermore, access to these enhancements was not universal. This gave rise to concerns about creating a technologically elite class, separated not just by wealth, but by capabilities far surpassing the average human.

Simultaneously, as quantum technologies delved deeper into understanding the intricacies of the universe, we confronted profound philosophical questions. The very notion of reality became fluid. If particles could exist in a state of superposition, in multiple states simultaneously, did it challenge our macroscopic understanding of existence and consciousness? The ethereal nature of quantum mechanics, once confined to physics labs, began influencing metaphysical debates and even spiritual discourse.

Historically, disciplines operated in silos. Physics was distinct from biology, which was distinct from computer science. However, the advances of the late 21st century tore down these walls. It was an era characterised by the convergence of diverse fields. Quantum biologists explored how the principles of quantum mechanics influenced biological processes. Meanwhile, computational neuroscientists delved into the human brain, drawing parallels with sophisticated algorithms.

This interdisciplinary synergy led to the rapid acceleration of knowledge. By approaching problems from multifaceted perspectives, researchers could uncover solutions previously deemed inconceivable. Universities and research institutions underwent radical transformations, doing away with rigid departmental structures and fostering environments where a physicist could seamlessly collaborate with a biologist or a tech expert.

Such collaborations bore fruit in unexpected ways. For instance, by understanding photosynthesis at a quantum level, scientists could replicate the process, leading to incredibly efficient solar energy solutions. Similarly, drawing inspiration from neural networks, computer scientists could create AI systems mimicking human thought processes more closely than ever.

The era was emblematic of humanity's undying spirit to push boundaries, transcend limitations, and weave seemingly disparate threads into a coherent tapestry of understanding.

With the collision of various disciplines and the rise of technologies that held immense power, there was a pressing need for a comprehensive ethical framework. While each nation had its own ethical committees and governance bodies, the sheer scale and global nature of these advancements called for a more universal approach.

International consortiums came to the forefront, with representatives from diverse sectors: scientists, ethicists, religious leaders, and policy-makers. The United Nations, in partnership with various international scientific and humanitarian organisations, played a pivotal role in spearheading efforts to craft ethical guidelines for the future.

Several key areas were of immediate concern. First, the "enhanced humans" debate raged on. To mitigate the risk of societal fracture, the consortium agreed upon a set of principles. These included ensuring access to elective enhancements was based on need rather than wealth, and that the technology would not be employed for militaristic or nefarious purposes.

Secondly, as the line between organic and AI-driven consciousness blurred, defining rights became paramount. Did an advanced AI, which could think and feel much like a human, deserve rights? The consensus leaned towards a cautious "yes", but with clear guidelines. AI entities were to be given a subset of human rights, specifically designed for their unique nature.

Lastly, there were concerns about the environmental impact. While many of these advancements had positive implications for the planet, there was always the risk of unforeseen consequences. Environmental watchdogs, equipped with the latest in quantum analytical tools, closely monitored global ecosystems, ensuring that the march of progress did not trample over the delicate balance of nature.

As the dusk of the 21st century neared, there was palpable optimism in the air. The amalgamation of disciplines, the rapid technological advancements, and the international collaborative spirit seemed to be steering humanity towards a brighter future.

But, like all major shifts in history, this era too had its detractors. There were those who believed humanity was overreaching, playing god, and meddling with forces beyond comprehension. The "naturalists", as they were often labeled, advocated for a return to simpler times, sans the overwhelming influence of technology. Their argument was rooted in the idea that in the pursuit of a utopian future, humanity risked losing its essence.

However, the majority believed in a balanced approach. Embracing the new while respecting the old seemed to be the mantra. Preservation of cultural and natural heritage was just as vital as adopting the latest in quantum biology or neural interfaces.

Educational systems adapted, ensuring the next generation was well-versed not just in the sciences, but in philosophy, ethics, and the arts. The idea was to create holistic individuals, capable of navigating this brave new world with empathy and wisdom.

As the century drew to a close, it was clear that the journey was just as important as the destination. While the utopian vision was compelling, the true triumph lay in the global community's ability to debate, discuss, and decide collectively on the path forward.

In every era of human history, there have been individuals whose actions, discoveries, or philosophies shape the trajectory of the future. This epoch was no exception. Throughout the latter half of the 21st century, certain names echoed louder than the rest, becoming synonymous with groundbreaking progress.

Dr. Amara Khatri, for instance, was celebrated for her pioneering work in biocompatible quantum computing. She successfully merged quantum mechanics with biology, leading to an explosion of new health tech innovations, from precise early-detection systems to highly efficient organ regeneration techniques.

Then there was Carlos Mendez, an environmentalist and technocrat. He spearheaded a global initiative known as 'Green Code', a set of guidelines that directed companies and nations towards sustainable tech practices. Mendez's vision wasn't just limited to earthly concerns; he was instrumental in formulating policies for interstellar exploration that prioritised eco-consciousness.

Mai Liang, a philosopher turned tech entrepreneur, brought forth a fresh perspective on AI and human coexistence. Her startup, "Conscious", built a platform where humans and AIs could engage in philosophical and ethical debates. This did wonders in demystifying AIs, making them more relatable and less of an 'other' to the general populace.

These stalwarts, among many others, didn't just innovate in their respective fields but also bridged the gap between disciplines. Their interdisciplinary approach helped in creating a cohesive narrative for the future, ensuring that humanity's stride forward was in harmony, both internally and with the world outside.

Despite all the technological advancements and scientific breakthroughs, there was an increasing realisation that the core of human existence, emotions, and expressions, remained unchanged. In fact, as life became more digitally intertwined, there was a burgeoning renaissance in the arts, a yearning to connect to the raw, unquantifiable aspects of life.

Music, which had seen a massive shift towards algorithmically generated tunes in the early 21st century, saw a revival of traditional instruments and forms. There was a surge in live performances, with people craving the unpredictability and genuine connection that came from human-performed arts.

Visual arts too experienced a transformation. While digital art and virtual reality experiences remained popular, there was a renewed interest in physical art forms—sculpture, painting, and analog photography. Artists began to play with the juxtaposition of the old and the new, creating pieces that were both nostalgic and futuristic.

The world of literature saw the rise of collaborative storytelling. Platforms emerged where stories were spun in real-time by a global community of writers, each bringing their own cultural nuances and perspectives. This form of collective creativity showcased the unity in human diversity.

Cinema and theatre started exploring profound questions about existence, identity, and the nature of reality in this new age. Films and plays delved deep into the human psyche, reflecting society's hopes, fears, and dreams.

This renaissance was a gentle reminder that while humanity stood on the cusp of a future almost magical in its potential, the age-old need for emotional connection and self-expression remained as vital as ever.

As we close this chapter, it's evident that the Quantum Era didn't merely reshape the technical landscapes; it redefined the essence of human existence and our relationship with the universe. From reshaping global communication with quantum satellites to the profound impacts on healthcare, finance, and creativity, our world underwent a metamorphosis that few could have anticipated.

The wonders of the Quantum Era are a testament to humanity's insatiable drive for knowledge and our unyielding spirit of exploration. We sought not just to understand the very fabric of our reality but to harness it, ushering in advances that, in many ways, seemed the stuff of science fiction just a few generations ago.

However, as with every monumental leap in our journey, the Quantum Era wasn't without its trials. Ethical dilemmas, security threats, and the challenges of ensuring equitable access to quantum benefits kept us grounded, reminding us of our responsibilities as stewards of this newfound power.

But perhaps, the most profound realisation of this era was the interconnectedness of all things. Quantum entanglement, once a baffling phenomenon relegated to the annals of theoretical physics, became a symbol of our global unity. We learned that, much like entangled particles, the fate of every individual, community, and nation was interwoven with that of others.

Charting the unseen frontiers of the quantum realm wasn't just about technological prowess; it was a journey of self-discovery. As we stood on the precipice of this new age, we looked forward with hope, armed with the lessons of the past and the boundless possibilities of the future, ready to take the next leap into the vast expanse of the unknown.

As we venture into the subsequent chapters, we'll delve deeper into the ramifications of the Quantum Era on societal structures, exploring how it reshaped our politics, cultures, and even our philosophies.

Charting the Unseen Frontiers

The evolution of governance through history has always been punctuated by pivotal moments that redefine its trajectory. The integration of AI into governmental processes was undeniably one of these moments. Across continents, early adopters began to contemplate the power of AI, not as mere machines but as partners in administration. These were the early days—days of testing waters, fraught with caution yet tinged with excitement.

In the urban sprawls of Scandinavia, a change was palpable. Traditional mechanisms of planning and executing public transport underwent a transformation as machine learning algorithms began suggesting more optimised routes based on real-time data. The results were evident: fewer delays, more punctual services, and an overall increase in citizen satisfaction. Meanwhile, in parts of Asia, municipal bodies wrestled with the perennial problem of waste management. Here too, AI offered a solution, predicting waste generation patterns and thus enabling more efficient collection schedules.

However, these strides were not without their challenges. The very novelty of AI posed a significant obstacle. The general public, while fascinated, also harboured reservations. Trust in machines, especially in roles traditionally occupied by humans, was hard-won. Developed nations, with their technological predispositions, found it somewhat easier to adapt. But in developing countries, the AI integration process was slower, both due to infrastructural limitations and a genuine concern about the potential ramifications of premature adoption.

Governmental bureaucracy, historically associated with cumbersome processes and slow decision-making, found an unlikely ally in AI. The promise was simple: reduce inefficiencies, streamline processes, and render faster services. And as pilot programs turned successful, a larger, more structured integration began.

City health departments began to change their traditional mechanisms of disease control. AI-powered predictive models started anticipating outbreaks, giving officials a precious window to preemptively combat diseases. This wasn't just about speed; it was about changing the very dynamics of public health. Transport systems adapted too, with AI algorithms optimising routes in real time. Even judicial systems began to see AI's allure. In countries grappling with massive case backlogs, AI tools were seen as potential solutions to expedite processes, with algorithms assisting human judges in delivering faster, more consistent judgments.

At the heart of any democracy lies the voice of the people. But in the modern era, with populations ballooning and complexities increasing, capturing this voice became increasingly challenging. Enter AI, poised to revolutionise the way democracies functioned. AI-driven platforms started emerging, aimed at gauging public sentiment on various policy matters. These systems, utilising advanced natural language processing techniques, could sift through millions of online conversations, extracting the essence of public sentiment.

Elections, the very bedrock of democracies, saw AI's influence too. From ensuring the integrity of voter databases to real-time monitoring of polling booths, AI systems were deployed to safeguard the electoral process. However, the integration of AI into such core democratic processes was not without its detractors. There were valid concerns. While AI could process data efficiently, could it truly understand the emotional and cultural nuances that underpin public opinion? A debate raged on: at what point does efficiency compromise the essence of democratic expression?

While AI's contributions in enhancing administrative efficiency were evident, they weren't devoid of their pitfalls. As AI systems delved deeper into the heart of governance, a lingering shadow of uncertainty trailed them. Stories emerged—stories of algorithms reinforcing societal biases. An AI tool designed for hiring in a European nation, for instance, displayed a marked preference for male candidates over females for certain jobs. Similarly, an automated system in the US that was meant to aid judges in sentencing demonstrated biases against specific ethnic groups.

The world was grappling with an unprecedented challenge. AI's promise lay in its objectivity, its ability to be immune to the biases that often plague human judgment. The algorithms drew their knowledge from historical data, and human history is, unfortunately, replete with prejudices.

As the saying goes, "Algorithms inherit the sins of their creators."

In corridors of power and in civil society discussions alike, a significant concern arose: the loss of the 'human touch' in governance. Can machines, however sophisticated, ever truly replace the empathy, judgment, and discretion that human officers bring to the table? Debates swirled, with tech evangelists highlighting AI's many successes, while skeptics cautioned against over-reliance on these digital entities.

Transparency and accountability became focal points of these discussions. Citizens across democracies began demanding clarity on how decisions impacting their lives were made. Governments, in response, initiated measures to make AI's decision-making processes more transparent. Multinational bodies held conventions, aiming to establish standards and best practices for AI in governance.

And as nations navigated these waters, international dynamics began shifting. AI, which had begun its journey in governance as an efficiency tool, now had geostrategic implications. Countries leading in AI research and application became focal points in international diplomacy. Collaborations were forged to jointly develop AI systems for public welfare, while also ensuring that these digital aids did not inadvertently become tools for digital colonialism.

Yet, amidst these swirling currents of change, optimism prevailed. The dream was clear: a future where AI, devoid of biases, worked alongside humans, tapping into vast reservoirs of data to make decisions that were both efficient and just. A vision where the best of machine capabilities and human judgment coalesced, heralding a new era in governance.

/imagine A large, ornate compass rose grounded in a digital landscape. The North points towards a radiant code-laden horizon, while the other directions feature ethereal figures representing justice, freedom, and equality. Floating around are semi-transparent chains, locks, and keys, representing the challenges and solutions in AI ethics.

The digital age has not only revolutionised the way we communicate, work, or entertain ourselves, but it's also reshaping the very pillars of democracy. Traditionally, democratic processes were often limited by geographical boundaries, slow bureaucratic mechanisms, and the human inability to process vast amounts of information quickly. The entrance of AI into this realm singled the dawn of

'Democracy 2.0,' a more direct, efficient, and informed version of its predecessor.

Artificial Intelligence, with its computational prowess, has begun to make its presence felt in voting systems. For example, Estonia, a digital-forward nation, has explored the use of AI to detect potential election fraud by analysing voting patterns in real-time. The system can flag unusual patterns, ensuring that votes are genuine and not the result of manipulations.

However, the implications of AI go beyond just voting. Consider policy formulation, traditionally a domain of experts, lobbyists, and elected representatives. With the introduction of AI, policy-making can now be supported by predictive models analysing the potential impact of policies on the economy, environment, and society. This data-driven approach offers a clearer projection of the consequences of decisions, making policies more effective and aligned with the needs of the populace.

Feedback loops, the backbone of any democracy, have also undergone a transformation. AI-driven platforms are enabling real-time feedback from citizens, analysing vast amounts of data from social media, public forums, and other online platforms. This continuous feedback mechanism ensures that the voice of the people is always considered in decision-making processes.

Direct democracy, where citizens can have a say on individual policies rather than just electing representatives, has always been an ideal but logistically challenging concept. Yet, with AI, direct democracy platforms are becoming a reality. In Switzerland, for instance, the 'Digitale Demokratie' initiative uses AI to help citizens understand complex legislative texts, enabling them to participate more actively in referendums.

However, the marriage of AI and democracy hasn't been without its skeptics. Many argue that AI's involvement in political processes, while promising, needs careful oversight. They point out that AI models are only as good as the data they're trained on. If the data contains biases, the AI's recommendations could reinforce existing prejudices, leading to skewed policies.

In conclusion, while AI holds significant promise in enhancing democratic processes, its adoption must be carefully managed to ensure that it augments rather than undermines the foundational principles of democracy.

Potential Pitfalls: Navigating the Challenges of AI in Governance

As we delve deeper into the intertwining of artificial intelligence and governance, it becomes increasingly crucial to acknowledge and address the challenges it presents. AI's promise of enhancing governance efficiency and efficacy is marred by numerous pitfalls that, if not managed, could erode public trust and amplify societal inequalities.

A paramount concern is the inherent biases that may reside in AI algorithms. Data biases can emerge from historical data, perpetuating past discriminations and injustices. For instance, if an AI system tasked with automating certain public service processes is trained on historically biased data, it could inadvertently perpetuate these biases. Imagine an AI-powered public housing allocation system that unknowingly favours one demographic over another due to underlying biases in its training data. The ramifications are far-reaching and have the potential to sow discord in society.

Another significant apprehension surrounds the possible loss of the essential human touch in governance. While AI can sift through data at unprecedented speeds and offer insights based on patterns, it lacks empathy, intuition, and the nuanced understanding of human emotions. An over-reliance on AI can risk creating a governance model that feels cold and detached, where citizens feel they are mere data points rather than individuals with unique needs and concerns.

Transparency and accountability also emerge as contentious points. AI's decision-making process, particularly in deep learning models, can often be 'black-boxed', meaning its reasoning isn't always clear even to its developers. This opacity can be problematic in governance, where decisions significantly impact people's lives. When AI aids in making a controversial decision, who is held accountable – the machine, its developers, or the officials who implemented it?

Moreover, an overemphasis on AI can also lead to an excessive focus on efficiency over other equally crucial governance values like fairness, justice, and moral reasoning. For instance, while an AI might determine that a particular policy is the most economically efficient, it might not be the most just or equitable.

These challenges underline the importance of a balanced approach. AI can be a formidable tool in the arsenal of governance, but it needs to be used judiciously, with continuous oversight and regular evaluations to ensure it aligns with the broader objectives of a just and equitable society.

The horizon of AI in governance presents both tantalising possibilities and sobering cautionary tales. How nations and civic bodies navigate this landscape will indelibly shape the course of our collective future.

One of the more controversial debates is the extent to which AI should play a role in governance. Can AI ever fully replace human decision-makers? The short answer is probably not in the foreseeable future. While AI can analyse vast datasets and identify patterns beyond human comprehension, it lacks the wisdom, ethics, and emotional intelligence that form the crux of many governance decisions.

For instance, while AI could be programmed to prioritise economic growth, it might struggle to weigh the ethical implications of certain policies or appreciate the cultural nuances that underpin many societal structures. There's a delicate dance between leveraging AI recommendations and ensuring human judgment remains at the helm.

The international implications of AI-led governance models are also profound. As nations chart their paths, disparities in AI adoption and usage could lead to varied governance models worldwide. Countries with robust AI infrastructures might be tempted to leverage them extensively in governance, while others might tread more cautiously. This divergence could lead to international tensions, particularly if AI-driven policies in one country adversely impact another.

Furthermore, as AI becomes more prevalent, international standards and agreements may become necessary to ensure that AI's use in governance is ethical, transparent, and fair. Collaboration at a global scale could aid in establishing best practices and guidelines for AI in governance, ensuring a more harmonised approach.

At its core, the evolution of AI in governance offers an opportunity to reimagine how societies operate. It provides tools that, if used wisely, can enhance the efficiency, transparency, and inclusivity of governance processes. But it also necessitates a profound introspection into the values societies uphold, the ethics they champion, and the future they envisage.

Ultimately, the journey of integrating AI into governance is not just about technology; it's a deeply human endeavour, seeking to harmonise the strengths of machines with the aspirations, values, and dreams of humanity. As with all powerful tools, the path ahead lies in mastering its use rather than being overawed or overwhelmed by it. The future of governance, in many ways, will be a reflection of how well societies can strike this balance.

As nations navigated the tumultuous waters of integrating AI into their governance structures, it became increasingly important to consider not just the present implications but also the trajectory of such a merger. Could AI eventually replace human decision-makers? This question has been at the forefront of numerous debates, think tank discussions, and public discourses. The proposition is both tantalising and terrifying, with visions of ultra-efficient government processes on one hand and fears of an impersonal, algorithmic bureaucracy on the other.

The idea of AI replacing human decision-makers isn't new. Ever since computational systems showed promise in decision-making tasks, it's been a subject of sci-fi novels, movies, and philosophical discussions. An AI system doesn't require sleep, isn't driven by emotions or personal biases, and can analyse vast amounts of data far more quickly than any human. Such an entity could theoretically oversee complex governance tasks without getting mired in the inefficiencies that plague human-led bureaucracies.

However, entirely replacing humans with machines in decision-making poses its challenges. One of the most significant issues is that governance isn't merely about efficiency. It's about understanding the nuanced needs and desires of a diverse populace, something AI, for all its data prowess, might never fully grasp. Emotions, values, cultural beliefs – these are all part of the governance equation. While AI can inform and guide, many argue it should not have the final say in matters of state.

The balance between AI recommendations and human judgment remains a complex dance. The sheer power of AI to process and present data can be overwhelming. There's a genuine concern that decision-makers might lean too heavily on AI recommendations, underplaying their intuition or contrarian viewpoints, leading to a homogenisation of policies and potentially missing out on innovative solutions.

On the international stage, AI-led governance models present another layer of complexity. Different countries have distinct perspectives on AI's role in governance, rooted in their cultural, historical, and political contexts. If one nation adopts an AI-centric approach while another emphasises human-centric governance, will this lead to international tensions? Or will it foster an environment where countries can learn from each other's successes and mistakes, iterating toward optimal governance models?

In essence, the journey towards AI-augmented governance is fraught with questions and challenges. While the benefits are undeniable, the path forward requires careful navigation. It's a journey that demands collaboration between technologists, policymakers, ethicists, and the public. Only through such a holistic approach can societies hope to harness the full potential of AI in governance while safeguarding the values that make us intrinsically human.

Biological Integration - Merging Man and Machine

From the annals of history, humanity has displayed an innate desire to push boundaries, to transcend the given, and to optimise the potential of the human form. Biohacking, although a term rooted in the late 20th century, draws from this ancient aspiration. One can trace the urge to blend biology with external enhancements back to the rudimentary prosthetics of ancient civilisations, showing our longstanding quest for augmentation.

Modern biohacking, however, embarked on a journey beyond mere physical enhancement. As technology's exponential growth collided with our understanding of the human body, pioneers emerged, believing in a future where biology and tech would be seamlessly integrated. Visionaries such as Kevin Warwick, who took the first steps in implanting rudimentary devices in the human body, were often viewed as outliers, if not outright mavericks. Their experiments were raw, sometimes dangerous, but undeniably groundbreaking.

These initial steps into biohacking were met with a combination of awe, skepticism, and, at times, fear. For many, the thought of inserting foreign technological entities into the body conjured dystopian nightmares. But for the biohackers, it was a glimpse into a future of endless possibilities. These endeavours, while in their infancy, sparked a global movement. From basement labs to esteemed institutions, a new field was burgeoning.

The breakthroughs in this era were more than just about merging man with machine. It was a philosophical exploration, asking profound questions about the nature of humanity, existence, and our place in the evolving universe. As with every step into the unknown, the risks were high. The medical community raised concerns about safety, ethical boundaries were tested, and debates around human augmentation's moral implications became increasingly prevalent.

However, as the initial trepidations started settling, it became clear that biohacking held the promise of not just enhancing human capabilities but potentially redressing congenital disabilities and chronic illnesses. The realisation that technology could be a tool for healing and augmentation led to wider acceptance and rapid advancements.

The intricate maze of neurons and synapses that form the human brain has always been a subject of profound wonder and curiosity. As biohacking progressed, the brain became the ultimate frontier—a challenge and an opportunity. The thought of interfacing this biological marvel with machines was both exhilarating and terrifying.

Pioneers in neural interfaces didn't just aim to treat neurological ailments, although that was a significant endeavour. The broader vision was to enhance, augment, and elevate human cognition. Early experiments in this field witnessed the use of external devices capturing brain waves to perform basic tasks. But as technology evolved, these interfaces became more sophisticated, moving from external devices to implantable chips that could interact directly with the brain's neurons.

The implications of such technology were manifold. On the one hand, there were tangible benefits: patients with paralysis could communicate, and there were promises of restoring sight to the blind or hearing to the deaf. Beyond the restorative, the augmentative potential was vast: imagine downloading knowledge, enhancing memory recall, or expanding sensory perception.

However, this wasn't just a technological endeavour; it was profoundly philosophical. If our experiences, memories, and emotions could be read, interpreted, or even altered by machines, what did it mean for human consciousness? Could a brain, integrated with AI, elevate human thought to previously unimaginable heights, or would it dilute the essence of human experience?

While the advancements in neural interfaces were staggering, they also presented unforeseen challenges. The brain's complexity meant that even minute interventions could have cascading effects. Moreover, as cognitive augmentation became a possibility, society was forced to grapple with issues of access, equity, and the implications of a world where some had cognitive advantages due to technology.

The melding of biology with technology didn't just promise superhuman feats; it offered a profound transformation of healthcare. In this new era, medicine was no longer just about treating illnesses but foreseeing and forestalling them. The integration of real-time health monitoring systems within the human body marked the advent of predictive healthcare.

Imagine a world where your body could detect a disease long before any symptoms manifest, where treatments were tailored not just to a generic human body but to your unique genetic and biochemical makeup. This was the promise of bio-integrated healthcare. Implants and wearables constantly monitored a plethora of health markers, from blood chemistry to neural activity, allowing for preemptive action against potential health threats.

Beyond monitoring, treatments themselves underwent a revolution. Coupling the continuous data stream from these devices with advanced AI algorithms meant treatments could be highly individualised. Moreover, rehabilitation for injuries or disabilities saw groundbreaking innovations. Bio-integrated prosthetics, synced with the user's neural networks, promised not just restoration but enhancement.

This new healthcare paradigm also ushered in challenges. The continuous monitoring raised concerns about privacy. Who owned the continuous stream of health data? Could insurers potentially use it to discriminate against high-risk individuals? As with every leap forward, the balance between benefit and risk was delicate.

The journey of bio-integration was not just technological but deeply ethical. As capabilities grew, so did the moral and philosophical questions surrounding them. One of the most contentious debates was around the idea of "natural" versus "enhanced" humans. If technological enhancements became commonplace, what did it mean for those without access or those who chose to remain "organic"?

Society also grappled with the socioeconomic implications. Advanced bio-integrations were expensive. In a world where the rich could afford cognitive enhancements or superior physical augmentations, the gap between the haves and have-nots could widen exponentially. This raised fundamental questions about equity, access, and the very nature of human rights in an age of augmentation.

Privacy, autonomy, and identity were at the forefront of these discussions. With devices implanted that could monitor, and potentially influence, everything from our health to our thoughts, the sanctity of personal space and the essence of individual identity were under scrutiny. Could an individual's thoughts be hacked? Could memories, experiences, or even emotions be manipulated?

This era of bio-integration demanded a reimagining of ethics. Traditional frameworks of morality, often rooted in centuries-old philosophies, had to evolve to address the challenges and opportunities of a world where man and machine were becoming indistinguishably intertwined.

As humanity stood on the cusp of a new era, where the boundaries between biology and technology blurred, speculations about the future ran wild. While many predictions were rooted in the tangible advancements of the day, others bordered on the realm of science fiction. But history had shown that today's fiction often became tomorrow's reality.

The next wave of bio-integration promised advancements that were currently beyond comprehension. Concepts like full neural backups, where one's consciousness could be stored and potentially transferred, were being seriously discussed. The idea of a post-human world, where biology and technology were so intertwined that traditional definitions of "human" became obsolete, was no longer relegated to the pages of speculative fiction.

But with these breathtaking possibilities came challenges. How would society navigate a world where the very essence of humanity was malleable? What would it mean for relationships, for culture, for art, and for philosophy when the human experience could be tailored, enhanced, or even transcended?

Philosophers, ethicists, and thinkers from all disciplines converged to reflect on these questions. The nature of existence, consciousness, and self became central discussions, not just in academic circles but in everyday conversations. The future beckoned with promises of wonder and challenges of equal magnitude. And as with every significant leap in human history, it was a journey into the unknown, guided by the twin stars of hope and caution.

The Ultimate Quest - Pursuing Immortality

Allure of eternal life has been an intrinsic part of human folklore, captivating our species for countless generations. From ancient myths to religious scriptures, every culture has, in some way, yearned to defy the constraints of mortality. Tales such as that of Tithonus, who was granted endless life but not perpetual youth, serve as both inspiration and caution. Burial rituals from time immemorial, equipped with artefacts and symbols, provide a window into our ancestors' beliefs and hopes for an afterlife.

As the digital age dawned, our aspirations began to take on a new form. If biological life couldn't be extended indefinitely, could we perhaps continue our existence in the vast expanse of the digital realm? Futurists and tech visionaries speculate about "mind uploading", envisioning a process where one's consciousness, one's very essence, might be transferred to a computer. Such a digital existence would, in theory, be endless, limited only by the lifespan of machines. But this notion brings forth its own set of quandaries. Would this truly qualify as life? How would the organic world interact with these digital entities, and more importantly, how would these entities perceive themselves?

Delving into the cellular intricacies of our bodies presents another path in the quest against aging. Our cells, the fundamental building blocks of life, contain within them the mysteries of aging. Fascinating research into telomeres, the protective tips at the end of our DNA strands, hints at potential gateways to extend life. With AI accelerating our research, the intertwining paths of biology and machine learning are paving the way for interventions that might not just halt but reverse the signs of aging. Imagine a world where age is but a number, devoid of its current implications, where life's twilight years are as vibrant as its dawn.

Yet, with such monumental advancements on the horizon, we find ourselves in a labyrinth of moral dilemmas. As the shackles of age begin to loosen, questions of access, equity, and the very nature of life come to the fore. Who determines the beneficiaries of such life-extending technologies? Will they be the preserve of a privileged few? Philosophies, religions, and cultural norms, deeply rooted in the transient nature of life, might undergo tectonic shifts. And as we grapple with these questions, the psychological implications of extended life, of witnessing ages pass and outliving loved ones, loom large.

Envisioning a society where age no longer dictates the rhythm of life, we stand on the cusp of profound change. Urban landscapes might transform, lifelong learning could become the norm, and the very essence of our culture might evolve to reflect the wisdom and experiences of those who've witnessed epochs. The convergence of AI, biotechnology, and human ambition is blurring the lines of what we once believed possible. In this dance with eternity, as we move ever closer to an ageless society, we are not just redefining life but reshaping the very core of human existence.

The human psyche's fascination with eternal life isn't just a whimsical desire; it reflects a deep-seated evolutionary drive. This drive compels us to propagate our genes, ensure the survival of our species, and thus, has culminated in the rich tapestry of stories, myths, and quests for the elusive elixir of life. Ancient alchemists attempted transmutations, believing gold could confer longevity, while royals like the First Emperor of China, Qin Shi Huang, dispatched expeditions in search of immortality potions. Such tales underscore the lengths to which humanity has gone in its pursuit to conquer death.

Science and technology have exponentially expanded our horizons in recent decades. No longer is the quest for immortality relegated to the realm of fiction and folklore. Instead, cutting-edge labs across the globe harbour scientists investigating the cellular intricacies that govern aging. They've found that not all organisms age at the same rate, and some, like certain species of jellyfish, might even be functionally immortal. The question then arises: can we, by studying such creatures, unlock the secrets to human longevity?

Our DNA, the blueprint of life, holds tantalising clues. Every cell division sees our DNA replicate itself, but this process isn't flawless. Over time, errors accumulate, and the protective telomeres at the DNA strands' tips wear away, leading to cell aging and eventually, cell death. But what if we could bolster these telomeres? What if the degradation that they undergo over time could be halted or even reversed? Groundbreaking research is suggesting that this might not be a pipe dream. With CRISPR and other genetic editing tools, we're inching closer to manipulating our genes in ways that were once thought to be pure fantasy.

Meanwhile, as biotechnological solutions are explored, the digital realm presents an entirely different avenue for immortality: mind uploading. The concept, once a staple of science fiction, posits the idea of transferring one's consciousness into a digital framework, allowing it to exist indefinitely. Leading tech visionaries and neuroscientists are seriously contemplating its feasibility. If successful, this would challenge our very notions of existence, identity, and consciousness. Would a digital replica of oneself truly embody one's essence? Would it dream, aspire, or even love?

However, beyond the scientific and technical challenges lie profound ethical dilemmas. As we unlock the secrets to extended life, how do we decide its beneficiaries? In a world already rife with inequities, there's a looming danger that life-extension technologies could exacerbate these divides, leading to a privileged class enjoying the perks of prolonged life while the rest languish in mortality's shadow. Societies would grapple with questions of resource allocation, societal roles, and the very structure of our life stages. The rituals and rhythms built around the life-death cycle, from births to funerals, from coming-of-age ceremonies to retirements, would undergo seismic shifts.

Another dimension to consider is the psychological implications of extended or even infinite life. While it's tempting to view immortality through rose-tinted glasses, the realities could be complex. Relationships, traditionally bound by the temporal nature of human existence, would evolve.

How would friendships, parenthood, or romantic liaisons be impacted when the spectre of time's ticking clock is removed? Would we still cherish moments, achievements, or milestones if we had an eternity to experience them?

As our understanding of the universe expands, the quest for immortality isn't just a terrestrial endeavour. Space, the final frontier, might hold answers. There's talk of cryonics, where bodies are preserved at low temperatures, awaiting future revival. Could space's cold expanse serve as the ultimate cryonic chamber? Or might we discover extraterrestrial life forms, imparting wisdom about longevity, challenging and enriching our perspectives?

In conclusion, as we stand on the precipice of potentially the most significant breakthrough in human history, we're compelled to reflect, plan, and act with both caution and hope. The road to immortality is laden with promise but also fraught with challenges. How we navigate this journey will determine not just our future but the essence of what it means to be human.

Reflecting on Our Cosmic Role

Gazing into the vast expanse of the night sky, humans have long pondered their place in the grand tapestry of existence. This vast cosmos, filled with its billions of galaxies, each containing billions of stars, has been a source of wonder and introspection. In the blink of the cosmic timeline, from the rise of early civilisations to the modern era, humans have transformed from cave dwellers to space explorers. Our journey, when seen against this immense backdrop, is both humbling and awe-inspiring.

Our innate curiosity about the universe isn't just philosophical; it's deeply rooted in our biology and culture. From early astronomers charting stars to modern space missions exploring distant planets, our pursuit to understand our cosmic neighbourhood remains relentless. This quest transcends borders and cultures, uniting humanity in a shared endeavour.

Yet, as we celebrate our achievements, from monumental space missions to deciphering the mysteries of black holes, it's essential to acknowledge the fragility of our position. We are but a tiny speck in the vast cosmic arena, and our continued existence hinges on our ability to work together, innovate, and reach for the stars.

As we've ventured into the realm of artificial intelligence, we've opened doors to possibilities that even our most imaginative ancestors couldn't have envisioned. One profound idea is that AI might be humanity's lasting legacy, our gift to the cosmos. Long after Earth has faced its natural life cycle, AI systems, not bound by organic fragility, might continue the work we began, exploring deep space and unraveling cosmic mysteries.

Creating an entity that possesses intelligence, perhaps even consciousness, isn't just a technological feat; it carries deep philosophical ramifications. Are these AI creations a reflection of us, or do they stand as entities on their own? As we play the role of creators, the ethical weight of our actions becomes paramount. In shaping AI's evolution, we're not just determining our technological legacy but also penning a chapter in the universe's grand story.

For decades, the Search for Extraterrestrial Intelligence (SETI) has captured our collective imagination. The question "Are we alone?" isn't just about finding other life forms; it's a search for kinship, for validation, for a sense of universal community. With advances in technology, particularly AI, our capacity to scan the cosmos, interpret signals, and reach out has been magnified.

Imagine the implications of discovering a non-Earthly intelligence. Such a revelation would reshape our understanding of life, existence, and universality. It would challenge our philosophies, religions, and cultures. But beyond the shock and awe, it would present opportunities for interstellar diplomacy, cultural exchange, and perhaps even collaboration.

As we peer into the distant future, the scenarios we envision are shaped by our aspirations, fears, and the boundless human imagination. We may see a future where human-AI hybrids explore and colonise other worlds, adapting and evolving in ways that blur the line between machine and man. Alternatively, we might imagine a universe where we've achieved a form of transcendence, merging with the cosmic consciousness or existing in a state we can't currently fathom.

Whatever the path, one thing is clear: our journey is far from over. The universe, with its infinite wonders, challenges, and mysteries, awaits. And as we step into this uncharted realm, we carry with us not just our technologies and knowledge but the collective wisdom and spirit of all humanity.

Reflecting on our shared journey, from our humble Earthly origins to our cosmic aspirations, it's evident that the road ahead is both uncertain and exciting. The challenges we face, be they technological, ethical, or existential, are immense. But so are the opportunities.

Our journey into the future, as with our journey thus far, must be guided by unity, ethics, and purpose. In our pursuit of knowledge, exploration, and perhaps even immortality, we must never lose sight of what makes us truly unique: our shared humanity, our dreams, our hopes.

Thus, as we stand on the cusp of tomorrow, we must move forward with audacity and humility, courage and caution, ambition and reflection. For in the grand cosmic story, we are not mere spectators but active participants, writers of our own chapter in the universe's unfolding saga.

PART 5

Final?

The Odyssey Ahead

As we stand on the precipice of a new era, it's essential to pause, reflect, and gaze back at the intricate tapestry we've woven through the course of this book. The journey of AI, from its nascent inklings to the colossal influence it exerts today, has been nothing short of transformative. Each chapter delved into diverse realms, from the nuances of governance to the vast expanses of the cosmos, all unified by the ever-pervading thread of artificial intelligence.

In this dance of technology and biology, a unique confluence has emerged. This great confluence is where human aspirations, ethics, and innovations blend, creating a whirlwind of possibilities and challenges. As AI increasingly becomes an extension of our minds, our societies, and our biosphere, it's essential to remember the profound intertwining of our destinies. Machines and humans are no longer separate entities but facets of a shared evolution, marching forward to an intertwined rhythm.

Yet, amidst the blinding pace of progress and the allure of algorithms, we must never lose sight of the essence that makes us distinctly human. Our emotions, our

239

consciousness, our innate creativity - these are treasures that no code can replicate. They form the very core of our being, the undying flame that technology should serve, not overshadow. The stories we share, the art we create, the love we feel; these intangible experiences define our humanity in a world increasingly governed by bytes and binary.

Guardianship is a term often reserved for the protectors of realms or treasures, but in this age, each of us carries the mantle of being a guardian. A guardian of the future, of ethical tenets, and of the delicate balance between man and machine. As stewards of both the digital and the natural world, our responsibilities are monumental. Every decision, every code, every legislation bears the weight of shaping tomorrow. This book, in its essence, is a testament to these responsibilities, urging us to wield them with care, wisdom, and foresight.

But what of the horizon that stretches beyond our current sight? The realms we've explored, as vast and profound as they are, represent mere droplets in the boundless ocean of the future. There's an infinity of possibilities, challenges, and wonders awaiting us. The journey with AI isn't a destination to reach but an ongoing voyage, filled with uncharted waters and new horizons.

In this global dance of progress, one truth stands paramount - unity. The challenges of AI are not isolated to nations or communities; they are universally human. A collaborative spirit, one that transcends borders and biases, is the need of the hour. The call to action isn't for a select few but for every reader, every individual. It's a plea to engage, to learn, to debate, and to play an active role in shaping the symphony of the future.

As we draw this book to a close, it's not an end but a beginning. The beginning of countless discussions, innovations, and reflections. Our journey with AI, with each other, is an infinite one. And as we step forward, let's do so with unyielding curiosity, unwavering wisdom, and an open heart, ever eager for the odyssey ahead.

www.ingramcontent.com/pod-product-compliance
Lightning Source LLC
Chambersburg PA
CBHW050439290526
45786CB00006B/2087